CRISIS-PROOF YOUR CAREER

CRISIS-PROOF YOUR CAREER

FINDING JOB SECURITY IN AN INSECURE TIME

PELLER MARION, Ed.D.

A BIRCH LANE PRESS BOOK
PUBLISHED BY CAROL PUBLISHING GROUP

This book is dedicated with love and gratitude to
my mother and father, Ruth and Bernie Peller, and
my husband, Ron Tilden.

A Birch Lane Press Book
Published by Carol Publishing Group
Birch Lane Press is a registered trademark of Carol Communications, Inc.
Editorial Offices: 600 Madison Avenue, New York, N.Y. 10022
Sales & Distribution Offices: 120 Enterprise Avenue, Secaucus, N.J. 07094
In Canada: Canadian Manda Group, P.O. Box 920, Station U, Toronto,
Ontario M8Z 5P9
Queries regarding rights and permissions should be addressed to Carol
Publishing Group, 600 Madison Avenue, New York, N.Y. 10022

Carol Publishing Group books are available at special discounts for bulk
purchases, for sales promotions, fund-raising, or educational purposes.
Special editions can be created to specifications. For details contact: Special
Sales Department, Carol Publishing Group, 120 Enterprise Avenue, Secaucus,
N.J. 07094

Book design by Stephanie Bart-Horvath

Manufactured in the United States of America

10   9   8   7   6   5   4   3   2   1

All names, identifying characteristics, and other details of the case material,
examples, and stories in this book have been changed to insure anonymity.

Library of Congress Cataloging-in-Publication Data
Marion, Peller.
Crisis-proof your career : finding job security in an insecure
time / by Peller Marion.
p.   cm.
"A Birch Lane Press book."
ISBN 1–55972–181–2
1. Vocational guidance.   2. Job security.   I. Title.
HF5381.M354   1993
650.1—dc20   92–39825
CIP

CONTENTS

ACKNOWLEDGMENTS

I am grateful to many people for their generosity and support during the writing of this book:

Candice Fuhrman, Barbara S. Brauer, Bruce Shostak, Ken Blanchard, Marsha Angus, Allan Prager, Barry Flicker, Susan Campbell, Erica Ross Kreiger, Victoria Barbaro, Shirley Griffin, Brian Moroney, Wayne Snyder, Tom Long, Gordon Smith, Tim Guertin, Nancy Cassaboon, Valerie Williams, Sally McCorgary, Barbara Block, Dhyan Bohnet, Tracy Carson Ferm, David Hayward, Meyer and Vera Baylin, and Dr. Tom Hunt.

I owe a great debt to my clients from whom I've learned so much over the years.

FOREWORD

KEN BLANCHARD, COAUTHOR OF THE ONE MINUTE MANAGER

I have known Peller Marion for almost twenty years. We first met when she was finishing her doctorate at the University of Massachusetts, where I was on the teaching faculty. I have found her to be a warm, caring, and insightful person. In this book, *Crisis-Proof Your Career*, she brings those wonderful traits into play on one of the most perplexing subjects facing everybody in the world of work today: how to find job security in an insecure time.

Why is this an important subject? The reality today is that managers and their employees can no longer expect the exchange of job security for hard work and loyalty. In this complex world, managers and employees alike need a strategy they can depend on. Peller Marion's book helps workers develop such a strategy for themselves. *Crisis-Proof Your Career* is built on the reality that there is no such thing as job security, but that capitalizing on your marketable skills and having a plan can create unexpected opportunities.

Men and women everywhere want answers to their career problems. Now Peller Marion's book can do that for you. It reflects a clear-sighted understanding based on twenty years of business experience that can help you to take charge of your own destiny and build a solid career strategy. It shows you how to go about identifying your needs, priorities, and goals. Finally managers and employees everywhere can answer the question so often asked in interviews (but often poorly answered): "What are your career plans for the next five years?"

The book is a result of Peller Marion's work with thousands of men and women with endangered careers. It is designed to help people of all ages understand why they are experiencing crises— including job burnout, dissatisfaction, stress, and insecurity—in their professional lives and to give them the tools to resolve them, especially in times of economic uncertainty.

You will learn from reading this book that a crisis-proof career lets you perceive many viable career options, know your marketable skills, and move forward with a practical plan for both the short and long term. A crisis-proof career gives you the flexibility, courage, and personal security to survive and even prosper in hard times as well as good times. Peller Marion's book can show you the way!

INTRODUCTION

*T*oday, millions of capable, hardworking men and women are on the endangered list. Previously successful and secure, these men and women now confront uncertain futures of unemployment, forced retirement, and dissatisfying, stagnant careers. Perhaps you are one of them.

Current statistics reveal the extent of this nationwide trend. In the last year alone, 9 million middle managers and professionals have lost their jobs. Within the next six months, another million will face unemployment. Millions more feel stuck in their positions, unable to advance or move to a different company. Not even in the Great Depression were so many educated businessmen and businesswomen made vulnerable to job loss and burnout.

The temptation is to blame the situation on the recession and changing world markets. The economy, however, is not the sole source of the problem. Periods of recession and depression merely compound endangered careers; they are not responsible for them.

Fortunately, even in insecure times there are steps you can take and options you can exercise to put an endangered career back on track. *Crisis-Proof Your Career: Finding Job Security in an Insecure Time* addresses the true reasons behind career endangerment and teaches sound career development skills that will enable you to survive bad times and make the best of good times. Based on my twenty-five years of career management counseling, this book provides a practical and proven program of personal assessment and development that you can readily implement to save your career from endangerment—now and in the future.

As an outplacement counselor, I have heard countless war stories from my clients. I have learned the various ways these men and women found their way into the job market and how they went about establishing their careers. For most of them, luck played a large part in their rise to positions of authority and success. They never had to develop their inner resources or answer difficult career questions. This is why they became endangered.

Larry's situation is typical. The company recruiter from a large manufacturer came to Larry's college campus his senior year and offered him a position in management training. That day marked the last time Larry thought about a career choice. Twenty years later, now in his early forties, Larry realizes he is no longer satisfied with his career. Yet he hasn't a clue as to what is wrong or what to do. What he does believe is that a career change in the midst of a recession would be foolhardy to attempt.

Lorna, on the other hand, went to work as a receptionist in a television production company after she graduated from college. She worked her way up through ten different production companies and is now a producer. But the stress and uncertainty of the television business is becoming unbearable. She's wondering why she ever thought it was so glamorous.

Crisis-Proof Your Career is written to help individuals like Larry and Lorna figure out what is wrong with their present situation and help them create a variety of choices they can exercise—even in depressed or recessionary times. It addresses the primary fears and career needs of workers who may be in the throes of crises of personal identity and job security by providing precisely the tools and information they need to successfully navigate this critical passage in their lives.

You will learn that a crisis-proof career is one in which you can explore many options, know your many marketable skills, and move forward with a clear-sighted, practical plan, both for the short and long term. A crisis-proof plan provides you the flexibility, courage, and personal security to weather hard times.

Without essential career management skills, even the best performers succumb to job insecurity. *Crisis-Proof Your Career* teaches these career skills, provides important diagnostic tools for you to determine your level of endangerment, and reveals the hidden reasons why apparently successful and established individuals face failure and insecurity, never reaching their goals but never understanding why.

In this book is all you need to discover how to set and reach your goals, and how to live by your own agenda—in short, how to crisis-proof your career once and for all.

CHAPTER 1

WHEN THE GOING GETS TOUGH
THE SCOPE OF THE PROBLEM

*I*magine a room filled with people who will spend a weekend together discussing their careers. They are men and women of various ages, mostly between thirty-five and fifty-five years old. One by one they introduce themselves and tell why they have chosen to participate in a professional workshop when they could be at home, spending the weekend with their families.

Within minutes emotions fill the room. Some people become angry, others anxious and tense, and still others have tears brimming as they speak. Why would such a rational topic as careers bring out such extreme reactions?

This question is especially puzzling because it is easy to see that these are competent people who have achieved a high degree of success in their work. They are presidents of companies, managers, entrepreneurs, professionals—all white-collar workers. They are recognized by others for their accomplishments.

Why are they here? As they tell of their reasons and expectations for the weekend, it becomes clear that each of these individuals is experiencing a crisis in his or her career. Some, victims of corporate

3

cutbacks or reorganization, have lost their jobs or are in imminent danger of losing them. Some are questioning the value of their work, wondering why satisfaction eludes them and what they can do about it. Recession, change, and uncertainty have influenced everyone in the room. All of them are eager to share their stories.

Sharon, a senior vice president of a regional bank, explains that she began work twenty years ago, at the age of sixteen. She tells the group, "My dad had a stroke and I went to work as a teller to support my four brothers and sisters. Over the years, the bank became my second family, and I've measured myself against its standards. I even met my ex-husband at the bank—he was one of my customers. Now everyone is getting laid off or 'redeployed,' the bank's euphemism for retraining and placement at a lower level. I don't know what to do at this point. Do I look for another job? I wonder if there will ever be any security in my life."

People throughout the group nod in agreement. Sharon has struck a common chord.

Bert speaks next. He exudes success from head to foot, but the tension is visible in his face.

"Everyone envies me because I am a management consultant. I live in the suburbs and fly all over working on strategic planning for corporations. My problem? I guess I've lost my passion. 'Follow your passion,' they say. Well, what happens if you don't know what they're talking about, because you haven't felt it in so long? I'd like to explore other possibilities, but the recession makes me afraid to look for something else. People tell me to hold on to my job, this is as good as it gets. I think they're right. Who would want an old dog like me after twenty years with one company?" He shrugs and shakes his head.

The next person in the circle introduces himself as Warren, marketing manager for an airline company. As he speaks, everyone can see how tired he looks.

"I'm a middle manager: middle-aged in midlife and midway to I don't know where." This prompts a laugh from the group and seems to help him relax a little.

"I was full of vitality in my twenties. I was all set to do whatever it took to get ahead. I was certain that hard work and brains would get me there. Somewhere I got lost along the way. I don't get very much enjoyment out of my work anymore, and I have another fifteen years to go before retirement. I came here for answers. I need to know what's wrong. Is it me or my job? Work seems to be getting harder, competition seems to be getting steeper, and my job always seems to hang in the balance. You know, one false move and I'd be out on the street. I came here to put some meaning, some perspective, back in my work."

The stories continue, each filled with pain and confusion about an uncertain future, stress, and dissatisfaction. The people in this room are typical of thousands, even millions, of American white-collar workers today. I see hundreds of them every year in my practice as an outplacement and career counselor. They come to me for many different reasons, but like the people attending the workshop, they have something in common. They are people at an impasse in their careers, unable to generate options, unable to find fulfilling and profitable alternatives. They are what I call the *endangered species*.

People become endangered for many reasons. Some, like Sharon, have never developed a career plan or thought to reevaluate their career decisions since they "happened" on their first position years ago. Others, like Bert, become caught up in the drive to "have it all." But despite everything they've gained, something is still missing. Or, perhaps, like Warren, they are working as hard as they can, but without knowing why, without personal satisfaction or meaning in their work. The result of these and a host of other career ills is endangerment.

First, let's look at how we arrived where we are today, and why so many hardworking, competent people are suddenly on the endangered list.

IS IT THE RECESSION?

Many people today blame their situation on the recession. Certainly the recession has affected us all. Since 1990 more than 9 million white-collar workers have been laid off or fired from their companies. Another 1 million will experience job loss in the months ahead.

It is a mistake, however, to think that the economy or any other single factor in the market today is entirely responsible for endangering people's careers. Endangerment is the product of internal as well as external factors. Let's consider the internal factors first.

AN ERA OF GREAT EXPECTATIONS

Those of us born between 1946 and 1964 belong to the Baby Boom Generation. Most of us Baby Boomers inherited high hopes and a belief in our limited potential for achievement. Our childhood was a time of expansion and prosperity in America. The Depression and World War II were over. Technology and the economy were on the upswing. I remember being the first on our block to have a black-and-white television. It arrived the same day my dad brought home our new car—a black Buick. In these and other ways, our parents communicated their big dreams to us, giving us a message about success and the material rewards it offers. Most of us bought it.

As young adults we set out to work hard and fulfill those dreams. Yet, after years of being in the work world, acquiring a work identity, proving our competence, and in return, garnering the signs and symbols of success, we now sense that something is wrong. We discover that our parents didn't tell us about the trade-offs we make for success. Perhaps, children of the Depression era, they didn't understand it themselves.

Frequently, the trade-offs are not apparent to us for many years. Bart, at forty-two, is just beginning to realize the high price he paid for his success. As a young man, Bart had no money for college, but his parents encouraged him to believe that he could become successful in spite of that. When Bart moved to San Francisco in his twenties, he enrolled in a career-track management-trainee program. This wasn't the liberal arts education he had wanted, but his parents back in Virginia were proud to tell their neighbors, "Our son Bart is a banker in San Francisco."

Years later, Bart is a successful banker, unhappy with his life. He came to talk with me about his growing uneasiness with his career and told me that he now knows he paid too great a price for living someone else's idea of success and never exploring his own.

Jody is another Baby Boomer who fell prey to high expectations as a young woman. Like many of her liberated generation, Jody has an excellent, high-paying job, a good marriage, and two preschool-age children. Her friends tell her that she "does it all." Yet each day as Jody drops off her children at the all-day child-care center, she wonders if she will regret not having spent more time with her children when they were young. She is perpetually exhausted and feels anxious about the choices she has made. She knows that something is wrong, but she doesn't know how to correct it.

These are two examples of the ways in which we've become a generation of outwardly oriented people, frustrated by our inability to acquire all the visible symbols and satisfactions of success, and still striving because we don't know what else will nourish us. Many of us have surpassed our parents' expectations and our own, only to find that the territory beyond is empty. What else? What will fill the void?

Jeff was a real go-getter, a self-made man. The first time I met him, he quipped, "No one on their deathbed has ever said, 'I should have spent more time in the office.'" He was in earnest, however, when he told me he was tired of being a workaholic. He knew there was more to life than his work and success. Now he wanted to begin to find out what that something was. We agreed to begin by reevaluating his career.

One night shortly after that decision, he went home, as usual, at eight o'clock, ate supper with his family, and dropped dead of a heart attack. He had just celebrated his fifty-third birthday.

Now that we are, as Warren said, "midcareer in midlife and midway to who knows where," we are at a time in our lives, like Jeff, when we want to take stock of ourselves. This is a natural, even predictable part of adult development. Yet never having done so before, we find the process difficult. We may not have a clear sense of who we are and so constantly compare ourselves to others. We may not know our true gifts and instead waste our talents doing things that neither challenge nor excite us. We may not know how to make our unique contribution and instead spend time doing routine and repetitive tasks. Finally, we may feel that we have settled for less and have let life pass us by. We stop asking for things. Worse yet, we stop thinking of things to ask for.

Byron knew when he was growing up that he didn't want to live the way his parents did. He moved to a commune in Vermont and began a cottage industry. He and his wife made designer baby carriers, which they sold through a mail-order catalog. Life was simple. When the recession of 1973 hit, Byron was smug. City folks waited in lines to fill their tanks, but Byron, Irene, and their three children had decided long ago not to have a car. They rode their bikes to town. In the winter they walked.

One winter, orders stopped coming in and money began to get tight. Byron put on the only business suit he owned to go into the city to get a job. His wife said he'd be good in sales. A mutual friend suggested that Byron interview for a position as a commodities broker. Byron was game. During the interview, his friend told him, Byron should just keep emphasizing that he wanted to make lots of money. Byron took his friend's advice and got the job easily. For a year he sold commodities, although his soul was somewhere else. He was named top salesman of the year by his company. During that year, however, his marriage broke up, and two of his children had serious accidents. Byron made a lot of money, but he was miserable. He felt a deep schism between his inner and outer worlds. Not too long afterward, he quit and moved to California.

Byron wasn't wrong to look for a job to support himself and his family through recessionary times. With the failure of his business, he had no choice. However, before he took another job, Byron should have taken a close look at himself and his career choices, past and present. Without that, he couldn't know which elements in his first career had given him so much satisfaction and, as a result, didn't know what to look for in a second career. Perhaps what had made the mail-order business rewarding for him was the independence of running his own business, its small scale, or the pleasure of working with his wife. His job as a commodities broker had none of those factors.

Many of us, like Byron, feel confused because we never took the time to answer some very basic questions about ourselves. Questions such as:

- What are some of the people, events, and books in my life that have made a profound impression on me? What do they say about who I am?

- What are my gifts and skills? What are my limitations?

- Where do I want to make my contribution?
- What are some trade-offs I must make, knowing that I can't have everything all at once?

Our answers to these and other questions represent the foundation of a crisis-proof career.

A GENERATION OF FOLLOWERS

Compounding this internal crisis for millions of formerly secure and successful individuals is the fact that the economy has taken a downward turn. As a result of economic and political developments around the world, the United States must begin to think of itself as part of a global village, not a leading power anymore. American companies are being eaten up by Japanese, Korean, and German entrepreneurs.

Other changes are occurring. According to a research project conducted by ConsultAmerica, cutbacks have become a fact of life in major corporations. Three-quarters of the top 1,300 U.S. firms have reported the elimination of one entire management level or more. Layoffs are epidemic. The result is a "flatter" organizational structure, in which upward mobility is dramatically limited. Experts tell us the current vogue for flatter, more distributive management is here to stay.

With the downsizing of companies, many managers are having to do the jobs of three people. More and more is expected of them. If they can't handle it, they are simply asked to leave. Many are let go because their once effective managerial skills no longer match their company's changing direction. In this new climate, managers must be more autonomous and ready to manage more diversified operations.

As the number of career positions is decreasing due to organizational changes, the aging of the Baby Boom Generation is rapidly creating personnel problems unprecedented in U.S. history. According to projections, a 50 percent increase in the number of thirty-five- to forty-four-year-olds will swamp the available opportunities for advancement on the job. People no longer have the luxury of exploring new careers—today there are twenty-five candidates for every midcareer vacancy. By the mid-1990s, fifty people will apply for every promotion that opens up, and for every promotion that takes place, there will be forty to fifty people who don't get promoted. Millions will be crowded on the first rungs of the management ladder and forced to stay put. A generation that expected to be leaders will be followers.[1]

The competition is staggering. Bernard Brennan, chief executive of Montgomery Ward, commented recently, "Every time I go to a party, I get several resumés from guests the next day. It's not always wise to ask people what they do for a living anymore."[2]

AN ENDANGERED SPECIES

The impact of all these factors on employees is more stress, more burnout, and more psychological withdrawal caused by frustrated career goals and life expectations. This is sending a ripple effect throughout many organizations. The "tree huggers," people who have remained after others have left, feel strangely dissatisfied with their success. They tell me that they feel insecure. For them, job happiness, meaningful work, recognition, and significance—all the things we achievers were taught to expect from our work—are no longer guaranteed. More and more people are becoming aware of the trade-offs. Most are having to run harder just to stay in place. A client told me recently that she gets to work at seven each morning and leaves at seven each night—that is what is expected of her. Even with a working husband, a stable job, and healthy children, she isn't happy. Despite her best efforts to appreciate her good fortune, all she can see is an endless stretch of twelve-hour days, week in and week out, until the day she retires.

Recent surveys report that twice as many middle managers are working weekends now as did several years ago. Over half think their peers are more stressed, 33 percent think their peers are close to burnout, and a rising percentage are opting for alternative careers.[3]

Marcia explained her situation this way: "I got married at thirty.

---

1. A multiclient study done in 1989 by ConsultAmerica, Inc., Concord, Massachusetts, "Outplacement Consulting in the United States in 1989."
2. "Where Did Gung-Ho Go?" *Time* (Sept. 11, 1989): 52–56.
3. ConsultAmerica, Inc., op. cit.

By then all my friends were on their second child. My husband and I were really workaholics and spent very little time together. So when I was offered a job in Japan, I took it. That was the end of our marriage.

"Japan was a whole new world for me. Life was slower. After working sixteen-hour days in the States, I actually had a life. I started to get to know myself. When I came back two years ago, it was really hard. I didn't want to go back to those long hours. I had some money saved, so I quit. I've been drifting ever since. I'm tired of pleasing people and being something I am not."

Many feel that the work is not worth the reward and are opting for a different work situation or a different career altogether. An alternative for some has been to move into small business, where the growth has swelled in managerial and professional jobs (by 6 percent from 1984 to 1986).[4] Others are reaching burnout and being forced to drop out and/or seek other employment. Yet this, as in Marcia's case, hardly solves the problem.

THE SOLUTION: A CRISIS-PROOF CAREER

Rudy Oswald, chief economist for the AFL-CIO, stated that "workers have a right to be upset and angry. They have been bought and sold and have seen their friends and relatives fired and laid off in large numbers. There is little bond in many companies between workers and employers anymore."[5]

Experts state that long-term upward career development and fast-track programs will be a thing of the past because organizations have fewer paths to the top. All indications point to the fact that it is up to workers themselves, not corporations or society at large, to take responsibility for their success. This means that we each must take charge of our own destiny and define the purpose of our career on our own terms. This is what a crisis-proof career will do. Does this sound impossible? Far from it.

Let me introduce you to two individuals who, like many, were casualties of current corporate trends. John and Tom had a great deal

---

4. "The New Executive Unemployed," *Fortune* (Apr. 8, 1991): 36–48.
5. *Time* (Sept. 11, 1989): 54.

in common. Both were in their fifties, both had been with their respective companies for twenty-five years or more. Both were unexpectedly fired from their middle-management positions.

THE OLD SCHOOL

John came from the old school of employment. He was known to say, "You just need one wife and one job, and you're set forever." He believed that the company would take care of him. John was completely unprepared, therefore, when his manager stripped him of his company badge and handed him a box of his belongings taken from his desk.

John went into shock. Like many in the same situation, he tried to persuade himself that finding another job simply required common sense and hard work. There was plenty of time to find something, he thought. He convinced himself that first he'd like to take it easy, just stay around home and help his wife with fix-it projects. With eight months severance, he could afford three months off. Well, three months drifted into six. By then, every door had a jamb, every faucet had a new washer, and every drawer in the house slid like ice. In the meantime, his severance had begun to run out. Despite his assertions, John hadn't a clue as to how to go about finding a job.

His first inclination was to do what he had done to find his first job, almost thirty years ago: he'd search the want ads. This was common sense, he thought. John saw an advertisement for a job at half the pay and several levels of responsibility below what he held formerly. He answered the ad and obtained an interview. The company's recruiter was polite, but John never heard from him again.

John repeated this same process for several months. He found it increasingly difficult to make the phone calls, write the letters, or face the interviews. Finally, a year later, I got a call from John asking for help.

WHAT WENT WRONG?

What lay behind John's "tough luck"? A number of factors. In the beginning, he underwent a dramatic loss of confidence. He wanted to escape from the trauma of being unemployed, so he stayed home. He used the excuse that he was being useful doing projects around the house. Although this might have been a positive decision for the short term, John let it drag on. Slowly it began to erode his self-esteem. John didn't realize that the longer he put off getting back out in the world, the harder it would become.

When it came to looking for a job, John didn't recognize that the job market was different from his first time around, nearly thirty years ago, or consider the fact that he himself was thirty years older. John's beliefs about the job search may have been true back then, but not now. John was a gray-haired man with more than twenty-five years professional experience, not an entry-level youth ready to be molded.

Because he had never anticipated having to make a job change, John had not built a network of people he could call on now for valuable information and support—for example, people who had left his company over the years, vendors, suppliers, neighbors, members of his church, or even a support group of others like himself. John failed to take into account that he didn't have all the answers. He never found out why he was fired. John was too ashamed to ask for help and yet was unable to manage his transition alone.

Another major impediment to his finding a job was that John didn't have a clue as to what his primary skills were at this stage of his life and had no assessment tools to find out. He was still operating by the outdated road map of his youth. He needed to update his personal values, take stock of his priorities and skills, and discover new options and choices in line with present-day realities. Before he went on interviews, he needed to know how marketable he was, what strengths he had that he could sell in the current job market. He didn't see that it was important to decide what he wanted to do in the next five years as a transition into retirement. Instead of making a commitment to a career, John thought only in terms of getting another job.

KEEPING UP WITH THE TIMES

Fortunately, Tom's experience turned out differently, although at the outset his situation was a lot like John's. The day he came to my office for his appointment, Tom was pretty discouraged. His boss had told him that his department was being reorganized, but Tom suspected that they were simply trying to get rid of him. On top of that, Tom had to spend the last week graciously training the new man. Tom's last day culminated with a staff meeting led by the new manager, to which Tom was not invited. Instead he spent the time packing his belongings in boxes. He carted these through the hallways to the parking lot. Feelings of humiliation filled him. He wondered if the staff saw him through the windows in the conference room as he fumbled for his car keys and opened the trunk of his car.

Tom was frightened, angry, and sad—and rightfully so. After all, this job represented a long period of stability and financial security. Tom wanted to talk about the disappointment and shock at losing his job. He was looking for answers and enlisted my help in finding them. He realized that to get the information he needed, he would have to ask some hard questions. Specifically, he wanted to know why he had been fired and what he could do to prevent it from happening again. He wanted to know how he should proceed with his career. Because Tom was willing to question his behavior, he could recognize that he might have to change a few things.

First, we reviewed the realities of the current marketplace. Unlike John, Tom saw at once that the job market was different from what it was when he had found his first job decades ago. I let him know what his chances were of getting a job that was equal or better than his last position. We explored the current trends in his industry and in his area of expertise.

Next, we took a look at a number of factors affecting Tom personally and professionally. Using a variety of exercises, Tom was able to analyze his current situation in terms of his likes and dislikes, career, and interests, and to determine his levels of satisfaction, stress, and burnout. We spent time finding out what experiences had had an impact on his career, his ideas about success, where he saw himself in five or ten years, and what elements would make up his ideal job situation.

By the end of these exercises, Tom had learned some important facts about who and where he was, as well as some facts about where he needed to go. He compiled this information into a preliminary plan of action, his Plan A—a new, updated road map to replace the one he'd used nearly thirty years ago. He laid out a plan for the short term that would see him through this transition, and a long-range plan for the rest of his life, his Plan B.

This made all the difference in Tom. He began to regain his self-confidence. He saw himself as a mature man with good judgment and a lot of experience. He still had almost six months of severance, and now, because he felt more secure and marketable, he was willing to take his time in making his next move. He did not have to be reactive or desperate or take the first thing that came along.

Tom decided he could benefit by going back to school for some refresher courses. He signed up for classes to update his knowledge of the technological advances that had taken place in his field. He even signed up for a few electives in areas he'd always wanted to study but never had.

Meanwhile, Tom adopted a daily routine that helped him feel better about himself. He joined an exercise club and swam four or five times a week. He spent some time each day on non-career-oriented activities and reading. With this breathing room, Tom was able to get a more relaxed perspective on his situation.

This facilitated our work together. Tom began to generate a list of options for himself. (I helped him look at corporate and noncorporate alternatives along a continuum of low-risk to high-risk situations.) We looked at what he would choose to do if time and money were no object and his success were guaranteed.

In anticipation of his future job search, we discussed his early experiences and how they led to his choice of career and his current feelings of fulfillment and unfulfillment. He identified important qualities in his work environment and the type of work he enjoyed most.

As we did this, Tom saw that certain beliefs were holding him back from finding the right position. He confessed to worries that he was too old and that he wasn't really manager material, after the beating he took. I suggested he talk to other professionals his age to test these assumptions. Tom drew up a list of the people he knew who could give him feedback about his age and managerial performance, including those who were doing what he hoped to do in starting his own venture.

Tom came back from these meetings glowing. He felt well received. He found out that some of the people he talked with had also been fired or laid off earlier in their careers, and they were willing to discuss their experiences. Next, Tom spoke with his former employees to learn their views of his work with the company and why he had been fired. That feedback helped by giving him a more realistic view of himself.

Tom was going great guns when he began interviewing for jobs in an engineering consulting firm. He wanted to learn all he could there in preparation for starting his own firm. He knew he had maturity, experience, and credibility to offer a new employer. Suddenly, he started to get cold feet. Every time he got an interview and the employer expressed an interest in him, Tom would doubt whether he could cut the mustard. When he told me this, we began to explore the self-defeating and self-imposed barriers he had about commitments. Soon Tom was able to see through some of the old thoughts about failure that were keeping him from landing a good job.

In addition, he began using visualizations to help him focus on positive opportunities. Tom wanted a job close to home, with little travel, in a high-tech field. I asked him to spend some time every morning envisioning the ideal workday. He told me later that this exercise helped him recognize the right opportunity when it was offered to him.

Tom took a job at a prestigious engineering consulting firm just five months after his layoff. The day he started work, he sent me a dozen roses with a card that said, "Thanks for the help. Believing *is* seeing! Tom."

That was five years ago. Just recently, I got a call from Tom. He and several others from the firm had left to start their own business. They invited me and my staff to the open house celebrating their new venture. "Everything is going according to plan," Tom reported enthusiastically.

A SIMPLE PLAN

In my experience, Tom's "luck" is not the exception but the rule. By examining his situation, collecting accurate information, reevaluating past habits and beliefs, and using this information to draw up short-

and long-term plans, Tom created a crisis-proof career. In the following chapters I will guide you through this same procedure so that you, like Tom and countless other clients of mine, can learn to live by your own agenda.

In chapters 2 and 3 you will find a series of exercises to give you accurate, concrete information about the trends and current forces in the marketplace and your particular level of endangerment in your present situation. You may identify some impediments in your personal and professional marketability and, by knowing what they are, can address them. You may find that your level of stress and burnout have obscured your ability to think and plan clearly, or you may have lost touch with the degree of satisfaction you want in your work. You will understand what elements in your work setting enhance your productivity. In addition, you will learn the critical warning signals that can alert you to significant changes in your company—signals that John and Tom failed to recognize in time and so were caught unprepared.

In chapter 4 we will consider many different forms of endangerment so that you will be able to recognize them in your own career. These include early life experiences that may have made you an achievement addict, holding on to potentially dangerous myths about success, achievement, security, and fulfillment. I can help you untangle them the way I helped Tom. Other factors include erroneous beliefs you may have about your work situation that can limit your ability to realize your potential. I will tell you stories of how others overcame the Belief Gap and how to deal with the self-imposed barriers that can handicap your efforts in finding a crisis-proof career.

Then I will lead you through the simple stages to a crisis-proof career. In chapters 5 and 7 I suggest positive changes you can make in your ways of thinking about your life and career and daily routine. In chapter 6 I'll show you how to put it all together into short-term, long-term, and fallback plans to chart a crisis-proof career at any age. These plans will be your own road maps to success.

In the last chapter, I will show you some examples of people like yourself who have benefited from this process, whether they started their own venture, went back into corporate life, or found a happy alternative.

Like Tom, you can decide that you are ready to grow with this transition and use it to create new dimensions. You can learn to take a crisis and use it to stretch yourself and make your own professional contribution however and wherever you want.

Let's get started!

## CHAPTER 2

TAKING STOCK

ARE YOU AN ENDANGERED SPECIES?

"*E*verything was going great. I was up for a promotion. Then suddenly things changed overnight. I couldn't believe it."

For the last eighteen years, Bud has enjoyed his work as a manager of a large New England utility company. Staff cuts and budget tightening necessitated by recent trends in the economy were tough on some of the newer hires, but Bud knew his own job was secure. He'd been with the company for a long time and enjoyed a good working relationship with everyone there. He took pride in being a hard worker who excelled at in-house team building. In recent years he was the one who presented the president recommendations on employee involvement. Even in the midst of all the chaos, Bud expected a clear sail to his retirement three years down the road.

As it turned out, Bud could not have been more wrong about his job security. Despite his unquestionable value to the company in the past, times had changed, creating important shifts in his company's operations. When his boss told him that he was going to be laid off, Bud was shocked.

Many formerly secure and successful people like Bud discover too late that they are indeed vulnerable to firing, layoff, and/or burnout—suddenly and, it seems, without warning. Yet there are ways to determine endangerment before the critical moment—if you have the right assessment tools.

Endangerment may seem to be a sudden phenomenon, but in truth it is usually the outcome of several factors—changes occurring externally in your job situation and/or internally in your personal needs and attitudes about your work. While endangerment may involve general trends in the marketplace, it also involves who you are, the choices you make, the priorities you set, and how realistically you go about acting on these choices and priorities.

Many people give relatively little thought to designing a career that meets all their personal needs. They approach their career one job at a time. In their eagerness to land the next job, they may not realize that they have the ability to increase their chances of finding meaningful work and decrease their vulnerability to job layoff or burnout.

Ian thought he could find the right job if he just switched employers often enough. When he turned forty, he realized with a shock that he was no closer to finding a satisfying position than he had been at twenty-eight.

Alice, like many others of her generation, panicked as she entered her thirties because she had no easy answers to her career questions. She felt something was wrong because her career had not been written on her name tag at birth. "How come other people's careers seem so straight and clear from reading their resumés?" she asked me.

"Simple," I said, shrugging, "we just rewrite their resumé."

We frequently leave our careers to fate when we could be taking action in our own behalf. Endangerment is a fact of life, especially when the economy takes a downward turn. Yet the decisions you make about your career are far more important than any trend in the job market.

The first step to take in crisis-proofing your career is to find out just how vulnerable you are. Some people are more endangered than others. In this chapter and the next I will give you the tools you need to assess your own endangerment.

In this chapter, we'll take a look at the external factors that can signal or contribute to your endangerment. First we will consider *Ten Crucial Warning Signs*. These are signals that my clients identified in retrospect as harbingers of significant new developments. Like Bud, most employees lapse into "it will never happen to me" thinking. As a result, they often fail to recognize the warning signs until too late. By being alert to these signs, you will not be caught off guard.

Next we will examine your marketability. *How Marketable Are You, Anyway?* tracks recent trends in the marketplace to assess where you stand in terms of the type of industry in which you work, your job level, area of the country, and so forth. You will see that in some industries, at certain times, and under certain conditions you are not as marketable as others. If you are currently employed, it will help you see whether you are as indispensable as you may think. How secure are you really?

The second test, *Your Marketable Personality Skills*, will match your personality to traits that land jobs and that are most in demand in the workplace. Too often, people rely exclusively on their previous experience to get them jobs and do not realize how much their basic personality matters in their career plan. This test illustrates this point by giving you a personal marketability score.

A crisis-proof career plan is built on clear-sighted understanding of your priorities, needs, and goals. In the *Critical Job Factors Assessment* you will isolate the set of conditions you need to perform at your peak and see how wide the gap is between your ideal job—where you do your best work—and your current employment situation. The test examines such factors as the amount of structure you need in your work environment, the physical setting, management style, co-workers, and so on. We'll follow this with a *Double Checklist of Job Likes and Dislike* from past jobs and then combine all your ideal job factors in two writing exercises: *My Next Ideal Career Situation* and *The Ideal Want Ad*. At the end of this chapter, you should have a picture not only of where you fit in the marketplace, but a better idea of where you'd like to be.

Before you begin, get a three-ring notebook binder, notebook paper, and a set of tabs. Label the tabs "Chapter 2," "Chapter 3," "Chapter 4," "Chapter 5," and "Chapter 6." As you complete the exercises, you will be instructed to record your answers for future reference in your notebook. Take a moment now to review the Crisis-Proof Your Career Plan Summary at the end of chapter 6. You will see that your answers to the exercises in chapters 2, 3, and 5 will make up the ingredients for your Crisis-Proof Plan.

TEN CRUCIAL WARNING SIGNS

Today everything seems to be in constant change. LPs give way to compact discs. Last year's computer software is hopelessly out-of-date. We have learned to take so many changes in stride that we may overlook some significant changes until too late.

Reviewing the following warning signs serves two purposes. The first is to allow you to detect your own vulnerability while there is still time to act. Ralph recognized three of these warnings right away. "I'd better get busy on that resumé," he said, "and renew some of those old contacts." When the layoffs occurred in his department nine months later, Ralph was already on the job at his new company.

The second purpose is to provide a sense of perspective. If you have been laid off, you may be caught in the past, fruitlessly searching for reasons for your predicament or blaming yourself or your employer. If so, this review can demonstrate that you are not alone and that many layoffs have to do with factors beyond the control of any one individual.

This was true for Marsha. After her layoff, she spent the next three weeks castigating herself, wondering how she could have been so incompetent as to lose her job. When I told her about the Ten Crucial Warning Signs, she was able to see that hers was not a unique situation. She could then step back and put some distance between herself and what had happened. Her anger subsided as she took a more realistic, less personal view of the situation. This helped her regain her confidence and look to the future.

These warning signals occur in three major categories: relationships, job content, and company performance.

1. A change in your relationship with your boss. *"I had worked for Phil for three years. Then over a three-month period things changed. What happened?"*

You have had a long and satisfying rapport with your boss when suddenly and for no apparent reason your boss withdraws from friendly conversations. Suddenly he becomes critical and demanding of your performance or unexpectedly starts excluding you from meetings and decisions in which you formerly participated.

2. A change in your reporting relationship. *"Phil called me in his office one day and told me I would be reporting to Rob, the new guy."*

After a number of years your boss decides to leave and a new boss is brought in to lead the work group. Formerly accepted as an excellent performer, you are suddenly subjected to rigorous scrutiny. Within ninety days your new boss is finding fault with your work and does not hesitate to criticize you. Some of this feels like nit-picking, and you begin to feel as if you are walking on eggshells around him. Your new boss may even criticize you in front of your peers at a staff meeting or shake your confidence in your abilities by criticizing you behind closed doors in his office.

3. A change in your boss's reporting relationship. *"My boss is not behaving as he used to. What's gotten into him?"*

Your boss has a new supervisor, and you begin to feel the pressure your boss is under as he tries to measure up to the new standards. Your boss no longer spends Friday afternoons joking and recapping the week with you before you both head out for the weekend. His door is closed most of the time. He delegates less to you and supervises you more closely than before. He is more critical of you. If you have complaints, you are afraid to bypass your boss and talk directly to the top man because your boss might feel undercut. So you suffer in confusion and silence.

4. A change in relationships with subordinates. *"My subordinates don't seem to treat me the same anymore."*

Your subordinates seem to be going around you for decisions and talking to your boss. They are complaining to him about issues they never mentioned before, perhaps saying that you play favorites, use fear and intimidation, don't exert leadership, or don't provide enough direction. All of your weaknesses suddenly come to light after many years of leadership and management experience. Most importantly, your boss is sitting up, taking notice, and not flying cover for you. He is now confronting you with this information. You are confused because you don't feel you're doing anything differently.

5. A change in job content—the job gets bigger. *"No matter what I did to distract myself, I couldn't stop mulling over things that happened at work."*

Your daily tasks are changed abruptly. Your work schedule may be overloaded already, but because you have proved that you are competent, you now have your job and one more besides. With each new responsibility, you feel more overwhelmed. Now you are no longer leading with your strengths, but sometimes with your weaknesses. Gone are the days when you went home at night and slept well. Now you wake up at three in the morning in a state of anxiety and wonder what fell through the cracks.

6. A change in job content—the job gets smaller. *"I can't help but feel excluded and I don't know why."*

Your daily tasks are abruptly changed. You are no longer responsible for major projects and operations that were highly visible and where you might receive recognition and rewards that would lead to promotion. In their place is routine and unchallenging work, given to you sometimes without adequate explanation. You are no longer invited to important meetings.

7. A change in performance appraisal. *"I was so used to getting 'exceeds expectations' on my reviews, it was a shock this time when I got the lowest one in my career."*

You have consistently received high marks on your performance appraisal, with regular raises. Abruptly, you are given a lower rating, although reasonable and adequate. You can't explain this downward trend. You can't get a straight answer anywhere. Your world seems to be shifting, but you don't know what to do to change your performance.

8. A change in the relationship with the parent company. *"All of a sudden everyone we knew from the home office was gone."*

The parent company begins tightening its expense account rules; decides on major cost-cutting measures for travel, vacations, expensed lunches; begins plans to increase earnings by reorganizing senior and international positions in the company; and announces plans to terminate major marginal projects, divisions, and positions. Stock prices go down. Everyone is grumbling, but no one is courageous enough to do anything.

9. A restructuring within the company or division. *"There were new teams and new divisions now. We all joked about how reorganizing made us look like we were making progress, but everyone felt a little sad for the old times that were gone."*

A management consulting firm is asked to come in to make recommendations about the efficiency and productivity of the company (or management itself assigns a special task force). The consultant talks to you and others about job content, responsibilities, reporting relationships, job levels, merit increases, salaries, grades, and years of service. You talk for an hour and a half, telling everything. Everyone else is doing the same, and management has all the information it needs to begin restructuring from the bottom up.

10. A change in the performance of the company. *"I heard it first at the water cooler: our stock was 'underwater.' 'There goes my retirement nest egg,' I thought."*

You hear news on the radio that the performance of the company on the stock exchange is spiraling down over a period of a month. There are rumors that there may be a merger in store, which means a redundancy of personnel at middle-management levels. Some people will have to go. You wonder if your job is really necessary.

Any of these warnings of instability in work relationships, job content, or company situation may not in themselves signify a cause for alarm—*if* they shift back to a stable condition fairly soon. However, compounded with other changes, they may spell O-U-T (of work) for you.

On a page from your notebook, list any of the critical warning signs you perceive in your workplace. From time to time, check back with this list and record any changes and any new signs. Remember, these changes occur over a period of time.

Crisis-proof people don't wait for others to decide the course of their careers or to act on their behalf. They know their options and have alternatives planned. If you recognize any of these warning signals in your job situation, don't wait. Better yet, act now *before* any of these scenarios applies to you. It is never too early to start crisis-proofing your career.

HOW MARKETABLE ARE YOU, ANYWAY?

Many people—and you may be one of them—feel vulnerable to job layoffs. Their fears are not unfounded. In recent years, American employers have trimmed more than 9 million employees from their payrolls. Futurists predict that companies will continue to be flatter with fewer management layers. Where does your job fit in this larger trend?

If Bud had taken this test, his score would have shown him that his position was not at all secure, despite his accomplishments. He might have acted sooner and found another position before he was asked to leave.

To find out your job security, circle the number on the left that corresponds to the one appropriate answer. Then total all the circled numbers for your score.

1 Your industry is:
(0) Utilities/health care
(1) Auto/retailing
(2) Telecommunications/chemicals
(3) Financial services
(4) Advertising
(5) Computers
(0) Not applicable

2 Your company's annual sales are:
(0) Small—under $50 million
(3) Medium—$50 million to $500 million
(5) Large—over $500 million
(0) Not applicable

3 Your company's market share or revenues:
(0) No recent decline in market share or revenue
(3) A current decline in market share or revenue
(0) Not applicable

4 Area of the country you work in:
(5) Northeast
(1) Midwest
(4) South
(3) Southwest
(2) West

5 Your company's track record on cutting employees:
(0) Never laid off numbers of people
(5) Already used voluntary-retirement programs
(5) Already cut some of the work force before
(0) Not applicable

6 Your job level:
(0) Line jobs
(3) Staff jobs such as management, accounting, finance
(5) Executive-level jobs such as senior vice president or general manager
(0) Not applicable

7 People reporting to you:
(0) You manage more than ten
(1) You manage between nine and seven
(2) You manage between six and eight
(3) You manage between two and five
(4) You manage one employee
(5) You don't manage anyone

8 Chances that your job can be done by subcontractors:
(0) Your job cannot be farmed out
(5) Your job can be done more cheaply on the outside
(0) Not applicable

9 Customer contacts:
- (0) You deal with customers frequently
- (3) You deal with customers occasionally and alone
- (4) You deal with customers occasionally and in the presence of your boss
- (5) You never deal with the outside world

10 How old are you?
- (0) You are under forty
- (5) You are over forty

11 How have your performance reviews rated in recent years?
- (0) You got a great rating
- (0) You got a poor rating
- (0) Your rating went up
- (0) Your rating went down
- (0) Not applicable

12 Transferable skills:
- (0) You are confident in your abilities to find a job across industries and relocate
- (1) You can't relocate
- (2) You can't change jobs
- (3) Your niche is small
- (4) Your niche is small and inflexible
- (5) There is nowhere to go

13 What is your profession or functional area?
- (0) None of the professions listed below or sales
- (1) Engineering, production, or marketing
- (2) Administrator of services

14 Your department in the last three years:
- (0) Stable, same boss
- (1) Relatively stable
- (3) Unstable
- (5) New boss within previous year
- (0) Not applicable

15 The general nature of your work is:

(0) Accounting
(1) Administration
(2) Engineering
(3) Production management
(4) Marketing management
(5) Senior management
(0) Not applicable
     Score ____ for your career

How It Adds Up

1–25: You are a pillar of stability and must be doing something right (like working for the government). If not, drop me a line and let me know how you've avoided all the turmoil around you! Unless you are very unusual, you may be fooling yourself. Your sense of security may actually be due to an inability to see the handwriting on the wall.

26–50: You are moderately vulnerable to the economy and the fickleness of the marketplace. Be sure to get started on a crisis-proof career before it's too late.

51–65: You are sitting on top of a volcano. It's time to do something before it explodes!

In your notebook, under the heading "External Marketability," list those factors discussed below that put you at high risk and those factors that put you at low risk of layoff.

What the Statistics Reveal

Industries such as financial services, banking, brokerage, and insurance companies are most prone to cutbacks, while utilities, local telephone companies, and consumer-goods makers are potential takeover candidates. Defense contractors and retailers are vulnerable. If you are in an industry that has already seen significant cutbacks, such as heavy manufacturing, you may be out of the danger zone. However, if you are in an industry that is just beginning to feel the crunch, you need to crisis-proof your career now.

What about the size of your company? Generally, if your company is large, it is more likely that management will be cutting in the future. Cutting is also tied to market share, which was probably the most prevalent reason for staff cuts in the 1980s. Even within individual companies, divisions with poorer market-share performance were more prone to cut employees.

Where is your firm located? In the last three years the greatest decrease in jobs has been in the Northeast, and the largest increases have been in the West. In the last three years, the top states for job growth have been Idaho, Washington, Oregon, and Utah. In terms of work-force cuts, a recent American Management Association study concluded that the best predictor of future work-force cuts was past work-force cuts. Of the companies that had cut staff in the past, 29 percent planned to do so again; of the companies that had never cut staff, only 7 percent planned future cuts.

Your job level is also a factor in your endangerment. Jobs in companies that face a leverage buy-out or merger are more vulnerable the higher they are. When two companies come together, there can only be one head honcho. Staff jobs are next. You are vulnerable in general management and administration-finance and accounting staff. Among the rank and file, it is usually the older ones who are given incentives to leave, so the new, younger (and less expensive) ones can take over.

The number of subordinates you have can also play a role in your endangerment. Companies that are reducing head counts try to get more managing from fewer managers. If you have only a few reports, you may be expendable. Today, the average manager supervises three and a half workers, down from about ten in the 1960s. However, today's companies are trying to increase that number to seven or eight people.

You are also more vulnerable if you use a lot of subcontractors or free-lancers in your division. Why should employers pay you a salary when they can cut costs by hiring subcontractors who don't need health or insurance benefits? Employers are making tough decisions on whether to farm work out or bear the cost of full-time employees. If outside contractors can do the job better and more cheaply than you, watch out!

These days companies have to be more customer-oriented if they are going to stay in business. So many companies are shifting their focus. This means that valued players tend to be those who have customer contact. If you do little else other than meet with other in-house people and write memos to one another, duck!

Age has always played a large part in endangerment. Forty-seven percent of unemployed men are between forty and forty-nine. Forty-four percent are between thirty and thirty-nine years of age. More than 60 percent of all displaced persons have been with their companies for less than ten years, 75 percent for less than fifteen years.

How are your performance reviews? This is a trick question, because performance reviews are irrelevant. A study done by the University of Michigan found that most employers view performance appraisals as unreliable predictors of layoffs. Everyone is skewed toward the top end and rated too highly. The pool of marginal performers appears very small, while the group that needs to be laid off is often much larger.

To survive in the 1990s, transferable skills are an important asset. The Bureau of Labor Statistics says that the number one skill in the American economy is the ability to adapt to change. Companies value switch-hitters—that is, people who are willing to relocate and who have many different skills. The reason is simple: when you still have 100 percent of the work and 80 percent of the workers, you want people who are adaptable and eager to work.

Obviously your profession and education play a large part in crisis-proofing. The highest job security is found in accounting, administration, engineering, and production management, and the lowest job security is in marketing management and senior management. Highest job security is found among technical graduates, or those who hold a PhD, EdD, or MBA, while those with the lowest security were liberal arts graduates or those who held only a high school diploma.[1]

Your score on this test indicates how you compare to others in the marketplace right now. However, there is another spin on this crisis-proof game: you can be as marketable as Joe DiMaggio was to

---

1. Amanda Bennett, "A White Collar Guide to Job Security," Wall Street Journal (Sept. 11, 1990): B1.

baseball, but if you have no motivation and the wrong personality, you may find security hard to find in today's marketplace.

YOUR MARKETABLE PERSONALITY SKILLS

Greg, a marketing executive, had what we call in the business a *boilerplate resumé*. He was a Stanford MBA and had graduated with a BS in economics from Harvard. He had worked for Procter and Gamble for many years. I felt proud to discuss him with my recruiter colleagues because of his education and experience. But he had no drive. How can that be? One recruiter put it this way: "He certainly has had his ticket punched, but now he has to generate interest on his own—and he comes across too laid-back. Even with a resumé like that, he needs to sell himself well. Frankly, I have other candidates who seem hungrier for the job than he does." In the end, Greg had more trouble than most finding a new position due to his lack of personal marketability skills.

What about your skills? This test is based on my research with four thousand clients over fifteen years. It will give you an idea of the kinds of attitudes and behaviors you will need to find the next right situation. Circle the number on the left that corresponds to your one answer to each question. Then total your score.

1 I consider this job search:
(1) A growth experience that I want to learn from and master
(2) A task I'd rather pay someone else to do if I could
(3) Something I would much rather not do

2 I think success in the job search requires:
(1) Using your resourcefulness and networking into new opportunities
(2) Having a high IQ and knowing the right people
(3) Having the right experience and credentials

3 When discussing why I am no longer employed or why I want to leave my present job:
(1) I feel I have a good answer
(2) I have an answer but I'm not sure I can pull it off
(3) I feel vulnerable

4 I consider myself:
(1) an extrovert
(2) an introvert

5 Rejection makes me:
(1) More tenacious
(2) More reluctant

6 What level of risk are you willing to take in terms of salary?
(1) A lot of risk—commission only
(2) Some risk—low salary and commission
(3) No risk—straight salary and small bonus

7 What is your financial picture?
(0) Not applicable
(1) My severance will last me for six months
(2) I have enough money to live for two years without changing my lifestyle
(3) Help! I have no severance and no savings

8 When was the last time you looked for a job?
(1) Within the last two years
(2) Two to four years ago
(3) Four years ago or longer
(4) I guess I was lucky—I never had to look for a job

9 What is your vision for yourself?
(1) I have a clear picture of what I want to achieve
(2) I sort of have a picture
(3) I don't know what I want to be when I grow up

10 How do you work a crowd at parties?
(1) I find three interesting people to talk to
(2) I talk to my spouse and people I know already
(3) I watch people all evening

11 What is your career plan?
(1) I have a written ten-year career plan
(2) I have a plan in my head, but I never wrote it down
(3) I don't have a plan

12 Are you aware of the obstacles you face in getting what you want?
(1) Yes, but I don't let them hold me back
(2) I prefer not to think about them

13 Do you have 125 or more people listed in your career "black book"?
(1) Yes, more or less
(2) What black book?

14 Do you keep a list of all your accomplishments?
(1) Yes
(2) I expect others to do that

15 How do you feel about being unemployed for a year?
(1) I am confident that I could use the time productively in my job search
(2) I would die of anxiety

16 How do you feel about calling strangers?
(1) It's fun
(2) It's agony

17 How do your friends or family feel about your not working?
(1) They would be supportive
(2) They would worry and hound me

How It All Adds Up

Add up your scores for your resourcefulness in the face of crisis. The lowest possible score is 16, the highest score is 44.

16–17: You are resourceful and confident about your career. Go get 'em!

18–25: You are teetering on the cusp of misery. You may be unsure how you are going to do in the job search. This book will help you increase your resourcefulness and resiliency in the job search.

26–44: You have a lot of work to do. It's time to get a grip on things. The next several chapters will help you change your attitudes about what is in store for you, whether you are still employed, unemployed, or just dreaming about a change.

In your notebook, under the heading "Personal Marketability," make a list of your strengths and a list of your weaknesses in terms of your personal marketability.

The Thrill of the Hunt

Looking back over your answers, you can see the areas in which your personal strengths come into play and where your weaknesses pose a problem. Let's review the facts behind the score.

People who see their job search as a growth experience and learn from their mistakes find jobs faster. They see the experience as an opportunity to learn more about their field, to meet new people, and to learn about themselves and how they respond to situations. In other words, they become enthusiastic about the process.

Crisis-proofers know that job seekers need to be resourceful and network. The job you want will not be handed to you on a silver platter—you need to go out and find it. You need to have a clear picture of what you want, with no inner conflict about whether you deserve it or not. If you don't, you may unconsciously transmit your conflict during interviews. You need to have a firm answer as to why you are looking for a job and feel confident about giving it. (In chapter 7 we will discuss how to get past the obstacles of self-doubt and lack of confidence.)

People who are more extroverted seem to experience less telephone fear, enjoy networking more, and on the whole seem to get jobs faster. Yet outgoing people are not the only ones who get jobs quickly. Quiet people also get jobs, if they persevere.

Tenacity pays off. For every one hundred letters sent out, expect to get one phone call requesting an interview. At this rate, it generally takes five and a half months to find a job at the management level in most fields. For this one response, you must call and meet people and put in a six- to eight-hour day.

Are you willing to take a risk, or are you risk-averse? Do you like to work on commission or do you need a salary and bonus to feel secure? It's easier to find opportunities—a desk and a phone—than to find a job. If you are willing to risk more, you can gain more.

The level of financial reserves you have to draw on during your job search can be a key motivator—or hindrance. Back in 1979, a client of mine was given $200,000 severance and outplacement with our firm. She had earned these through her twenty-eight years of service building the company. When I asked her what she wanted to do next, she said, "Don't call me, I'll call you when I'm ready to start looking for a job." I never heard from her. She probably put her money to work for her and is living off the interest.

Unfortunately, most of us are not so lucky. It is typical for a person who earns $80,000 a year, who is married and has a child, to have about four months' savings. That's it. Considering that it typically takes five and a half months to find a job, it is easy to see how important it is for you to maximize your time in the job search.

Most people underestimate the time and effort it takes to find the next right position. This is why I find myself cringing when people say, "I guess I was lucky. I never had to look for a job." "Luck" has little to do with it. People like this frequently start their job search with a severe handicap: they have some very naive expectations of the level of effort required to find a job. Most people who have looked for a job in the last two years, whether employed or unemployed at the time, experience a higher degree of confidence than those out in the job market for the first time in ten or more years. Experience gives them a more realistic picture of the process and how to achieve their goal.

Most people have a hard time creating a positive vision, yet envisioning what you want can be a rewarding experience. The cartoonist Ashley Brillant said, "Some of my fondest memories are of things that have never actually happened." Worse than not creating a positive vision is to imagine a negative picture of a future career. Some job seekers imagine pumping gas, cleaning houses, or parking cars. Frequently they imagine beginning again an entry-level job they hated. We'll address this problem in chapter 5.

Crisis-proof people develop a positive vision for themselves. Donna was a stressed-out payroll manager working in the tax department at a telephone company. She told me that she always felt guilty about not being the perfect mother. She'd like to work at home and to have a day of shopping and playing with her six-year-old daughter and her nine-year-old son once in a while. I helped her create a picture of being a sole proprietor and helping small businesses with their payroll so she could more fully integrate her life and her work. Once she started acting on this plan, her church became her first client. Then a wealthy church member found out about her work and asked her if she could do his payroll and bookkeeping also. In no time she had two part-time jobs, could work at home, and spent more time with her children.

Networkers are made, not born. Crisis-proof people love to go to gatherings because they are an informal and effective way to meet people. They decide that they are going to talk to at least three people, but they don't just plunge right in. They stand back, observe, and then carefully choose whom they want to meet. They initiate the contact by going up to them and introducing themselves. They might find a common interest by asking, "How do you know Bob and Sue?"

Unfortunately, most people don't have a serious career plan. A career plan is different from a positive vision; unlike a vision, a plan is linear and analytical, like a road map with all the exits and toll plazas marked. It shows you how to get there. It is essential to have both a vision and a plan.

Crisis-proof career people know that obstacles are a normal part of life. By accepting them and planning around them, they become excellent problem solvers. They make a list of all the foreseeable obstacles and then creatively decide how they plan to overcome each one (as we will do in chapter 5).

In an informal study I did independently with my clients (which was then duplicated by the Stanford Business School Alumni Club), I discovered that it takes 125 face-to-face contacts to find the next exactly right position at midlevel management.[2] No matter where you are in your career, you should start keeping a "little black book." (We'll talk more about networking in chapter 7.)

Everyone feels they don't get enough feedback. We all want to be filled with recognition and appreciation, but we must learn to recognize our accomplishments and not rely on others to do it for us. At the end of every day write down those small and large things that you like about yourself and what you did well. These accomplish-

---

2. My appreciation to Susan Gould, president of Human Resource Strategists and a Stanford Business School Alumni, who assisted me in this action research in the spring of 1989.

ments are grist for your resumé mill and for your conversations with people. They will also help you feel more confident about your job search and what you have to offer.

People who are optimistic tend to find jobs faster. They have more energy and follow up on leads. They tell themselves positive things. On the other hand, being pessimistic makes it harder to keep trying.

The telephone is indispensable to the job search, yet many clients have a dread of calling strangers or approaching acquaintances by phone. If this is your problem, relax. Cold calling is hard, but I will show you some useful techniques you can use to make these calls more easily—you might even come to enjoy them! But if you're one of those who find cold calls too difficult, I'll show you in chapter 7 how you never have to talk to a stranger.

Crisis-proofers surround themselves with people who are supportive of their job search and encourage them to find something they will really enjoy, not just another dull-witted job. They also find support groups of people who have other interests (but *not* unemployment support groups!). This is a time to take a class, one that nourishes your mind and spirit and puts you in contact with employed people. Join a dream interpretation group, or take a computer or dance class.

YOUR MARKETABILITY: THE BIG PICTURE

Now compare your score from How Marketable Are You, Anyway? with that from Your Marketable Personality Skills. If you had a high score on the first test and a high score on the second test, you need to work hard to overcome both sources of endangerment: difficult external conditions and your natural inclination to be risk-averse.

If you had a high score on the first test and a low score on the second test, you have a good chance to overcome an unstable career marketplace because of your resourcefulness in the face of adversity. This book will give you some tips you might not have thought of already.

If you had a low score on the first test and a high score on the second test, now is a good time to read this book, *before* you need it!

If you had a low score on the first test and a low score on the second test, you are in good shape. This book will help you sharpen up your skills for the future.

CRITICAL JOB FACTORS ASSESSMENT

Most people become very myopic when they work in the same setting for a few years. They begin to forget that they actually *chose* to work at that company in the first place. They begin to feel powerless, as if they have no choice over what they do and where they work. The longer they are there, the worse it gets. They begin to think that all jobs must be as dissatisfying as theirs. What's more, they begin to doubt whether they will again find satisfaction in their chosen career.

In 85 percent of all cases, the setting is the problem, not the chosen career. These beleaguered employees forget the crucial role that setting plays in job happiness. Stuart's case is a classic example. When I met him, Stuart was unhappy with his job as a financial analyst at a large engineering company. He complained that he rose at the crack of dawn, rode the subway into the city, and worked in an office that had no windows. In the winter, it was already dark when he left the office. Stuart was so miserable he contemplated a career change into the computer field. After completing the Critical Job Factors Assessment, however, he saw that it wasn't the work that was getting him down, but his work conditions. He realized how much he longed for a job that had more physical beauty and windows! How simple. He eventually found a job in the suburbs as chief financial officer for the county hospice.

Most people don't stop to define what is truly important in their job situation in specific or concrete terms. Often, like Stuart, they misplace the blame and in the end make the problem bigger and more complex. So before you plan to switch careers or move to another part of the country in an effort to find the right job, take the Critical Job Factors Assessment. It will help you define what you really need by pinpointing what it is that bothers you or what you need and don't have in your present job.

Write a number from 1 to 5 in the space next to each of the following job factors, with 1 indicating no importance, 2 indicating little importance, 3 indicating some importance, 4 indicating great importance, and 5 indicating that it is essential to your happiness on the job.

Critical Job Factors Assessment

WORKING CONDITIONS

Once you know what is important to you to have or not have in your working conditions, you can keep it in mind when going for a job interview, or look for ways to modify your present environment.

— Quiet and contemplative
— High activity level
— Large groups of people
— Few coworkers
— Nonsmoking
— Smoking
— Community work spaces
— Private offices
— No windows
— Windows
— Artificial light
— Natural light
— Individualized decor
— Uniform decor

In your notebook, summarize the important aspects of your working conditions by listing the top three.

REWARDS

Most people focus on the salary and benefits of a job, and not on other, less tangible rewards such as self-satisfaction and intellectual stimulation. In my experience, lack of advancement is the second major cause of job dissatisfaction.

— Money/financial potential
— Flexible time
— Increased vacation time
— Learning opportunities
— Self-satisfaction

__ Benefits
__ Being of service to others
__ Recognition/fame
__ Room for advancement
__ Perquisites—e.g., clubs, a car
__ Incentives/bonuses
__ Stock equity ownership
__ Travel opportunities
__ Power
__ Influence
__ Intellectual stimulation
__ Allowances, entertainment
__ Financial rewards steady, not tied to results
__ Salary plus commission
__ Salary plus bonus

In your notebook, summarize the most important rewards by listing the top three.

FEEDBACK PREFERENCES

Most clients feel that they never get enough feedback from their boss. On the other hand, bosses tell me they give their employees lots of feedback. I can't help but wonder at the confusion in this area. One thing is clear, however: feedback is important to job satisfaction.

__ Formal
__ Informal
__ Frequent
__ Infrequent
__ Regular performance review
__ Ranked against peers
__ Evaluated by mutually set objectives

In your notebook, summarize the most important feedback preferences by listing the top three.

HOURS

Rarely do I speak with someone who does not want to give an honest day's work for an honest day's pay, but who decides when the day begins? Whether or not we deliver our best on the job can depend a lot on whether our inner clock is in sync with our hours on the job.

— Start early, end early
— Start early, end late
— Start late, end late
— 40–50 hours a week
— 50–60 hours a week
— 60–70 hours a week
— 70+ hours a week
— Fixed, scheduled hours
— Flexible work hours/days

In your notebook, summarize the most important work-hour preferences by listing the top three.

PEOPLE FACTORS

The people with whom we interact daily also affect us. They may determine whether or not we enjoy our job or hate it. A poor relationship with the boss is the primary reason people give for leaving their jobs. Our coworkers often provide the sense of community and support we need but frequently miss in this day of divorce and frequent moves. Working relationships with clients can deepen into significant friendships.

Consider the People Factors listed below as you believe they should apply to your boss, your coworkers, and your clients/customers. Place a number in each column, using the same rating system as above.

COWORKERS	CLIENTS/CUSTOMERS	BOSS
Friendly		
Serious		
Sense of humor		
More experienced, so you can learn		
Less experienced, so you can teach		

Mixed ages
Interact with same people
   routinely
Interact with strangers
   routinely
Accessible
Inspirational
Culturally diverse
Nontechnical
Technical
Work alone
Team player
Casually dressed
Formally dressed
Mainly men
Mainly women
Educated peers (MBAs, PhDs)
Variety of educational levels

In your notebook, summarize the most important coworker, client/ customer, and boss preferences by listing the top three.

JOB CONTENT
What do you want from your job? Do you place your career at the center of your life so it consumes the lion's share of your time, energy, and attention, or do you want a job that shares equal time with family and hobbies? Is your job suited to your basic personality?

___ Routine tasks/predictable
___ Nontechnical
___ Fast pace/surprises
___ Slow/even pace
___ Planning/design
___ Assessing/evaluating
___ Little customer contact
___ Lots of customer contact
___ Project management

— People management
— Freedom to act
— Independent judgment
— Challenge
— Opportunity for novel experiences
— Nonrecurring tasks
— Varied tasks
— Physical labor
— High structure/goals set by others
— Low structure/goals set by self
— Absorbing job: think about it at home
— 9–5 job: leave it at work
— Work out of doors
— Stationary/desk work
— Lots of supervision
— Limited supervision
— Lots of responsibility
— Little responsibility
— Requires expertise
— Little public speaking
— Moderate public speaking
— Lots of public speaking
— Opportunity for creativity
— Specified deadlines
— Attention to detail
— Attention to "big picture"

In your notebook, summarize the most important aspects of job content by listing the top three.

PERSONAL AND PROFESSIONAL DEVELOPMENT

For many people, job satisfaction rests on the amount of enjoyment and stimulation they receive from what they do. What do you want your job to do for you?

— Build on current skills
— Open branching opportunities into new areas
— Provide mentoring

___ Continuing education
___ Give in-house training
___ Give external exposure and interaction
___ Provide productivity tools such as computers, software, etc.
___ Provide opportunities to become financially independent
___ Provide opportunities to develop peers and subordinates
___ Provide opportunities for adventure
___ Provide opportunities to belong to a team
___ Provide opportunities for power and influence
___ Provide opportunities for fame and recognition

In your notebook, summarize the most important aspects of personal and professional development by listing the top three.

COMPANY MANAGEMENT, CULTURE, VALUES
The values expressed and acted upon by a company are important to employees, who want to feel that their values are compatible with the company's. It may make the difference between giving 100 percent and giving only 80 percent, because you don't feel part of the team.

___ Valued group/division
___ Privately owned and run
___ Formal systems, policies
___ Welcomes change/innovation
___ Value tradition
___ Competitive environment
___ Cooperative environment
___ Centralized organization
___ Decentralized organization
___ Top-down management
___ Highly structured
___ Loosely structured
___ Socially responsible company
___ Hierarchical organization
___ Horizontal organization
___ Emphasis on integrity
___ Attracts top management talent
___ Professionally managed

In your notebook, summarize the most important aspects of company management, culture, and values by listing the top three.

COMPANY POSITION

More and more people are making the move to smaller companies, where they are afforded more autonomy and responsibility—if they are willing to take risks. One of the trade-offs may be that smaller companies can't always deliver the same level of salary and benefits as larger firms.

— Respected industry leader
— Industry upstart/maverick
— Widely known
— Relatively unknown

In your notebook, summarize the most important aspects of company position by listing the top three.

LOCATION/TRAVEL/COMMUTE

Commuting time is an important factor in our time-conscious age. Most people feel one hour is about as much time as they can stand to spend commuting. Traveling, too, is preferred in moderation. Most people don't mind traveling two days out of the month, but jobs with heavy travel tend to discourage employees, unless they are single, energetic, and young.

— Urban
— Suburban
— Industrial park
— Financial district
— Commute ½–1 hour
— Commute 1–2 hours
— Travel
— More than 1 week a month
— Less than 1 week a month
— 1–2 weeks a month
— More than 2 weeks a month
— Local travel in state

___ Regional travel

___ National travel

___ International travel

In your notebook, summarize the most important aspects of location, travel, and commute by listing the top three.

MOST CRITICAL JOB FACTORS
From all the preceding lists, select ten items you consider most critical to your job satisfaction and write them in your notebook under the heading "Most Critical Job Factors."

Now, rank the top five factors.

DOUBLE CHECKLIST OF LIKES AND DISLIKES
Now put the lists from the Critical Job Factors Assessment aside for the moment. Get a blank sheet of paper and draw a vertical line down the center. On one side of the line write the heading "Things I like(d) about this job." On the other side head it "Things I dislike(d) about this job." Start with your present job and list all the things you like and dislike about it. Next, think back to your previous job and do the same thing. Repeat the process for every job you've had in the last fifteen years, no matter how briefly you held it. Again, be as specific and concrete as possible. This is a good way to see if there is anything missing from your original Critical Job Factors Assessment. If there is, add it to the final ranking in your notebook. Then list all the crucial factors missing from your current job.

Use this list of crucial missing factors as a brief measure of the job satisfaction you are experiencing in your present position (we will examine other aspects of job satisfaction in the next chapter). If you feel there is a wide gap between your ideal job and your current position, you cannot play up your strengths. As a result, you may be unhappy, feeling as if you are an impostor, or performing marginally. All of these significantly increase your vulnerability.

Now take all the information you listed as essential to your job satisfaction and use it to write a description of your next ideal career situation on a piece of paper under the heading "My Next Ideal Career Situation." Be as descriptive as you can.

MY NEXT IDEAL CAREER SITUATION

It is _____ o'clock on _____ day and I am preparing to go to work. I live in a _____. I live with _____. I am getting dressed. I look in the mirror. I see myself wearing _____. I leave to go to work. My job is _____ minutes from where I live. The place where I work is _____. The immediate setting where I perform my job looks _____. My employer is _____. The kind of supervision I have is _____. My coworkers are _____. I have been working a few hours and it is time for lunch. The place where I eat lunch is _____. I eat lunch with _____. After lunch, I am back at work and continue working until it is time to go home. Some of my tasks are _____. I arrive home at _____ o'clock, in time for _____. After _____, I have a few hours to spend. Usually I spend the time by _____. Tomorrow I will be going to work again. The thought of going to my job makes me feel _____.

Stuart's example:

It is early morning on a weekday. I live in a house near where I work. I live with my new wife. I am getting dressed. I look in the mirror. I see myself wearing sport clothes. I leave to go to work. My job is fifteen minutes from where I live. The place where I work is ground level, lots of windows, in the suburbs. The immediate setting where I perform my job looks casual. It's an office, but expensively furnished and surrounded by other offices. My employer is involved in a humanitarian endeavor. The kind of supervision I have is minimal. I report directly to the president. My coworkers are educated, professional people. I have been working for a few hours and it is time for lunch. The place where I eat is nearby. It's a little cafe where I can have my sandwich outside. After lunch, I am back at work and continue working until it is time to go home. I arrive at home in time for dinner. After dinner, I have a few hours to spend. Usually, I spend the time by reading the news or jogging. Tomorrow I will be going to work again. The thought of going to my job makes me feel good.

THE IDEAL WANT AD

Now take what you've written about your ideal job and write a newspaper want ad for yourself. This is taking the same information and writing it the way an employer might describe you and the job you want. Begin with the job title and describe the years of experience, level of education, size of company, location, level of position, job tasks to be performed, and salary. Discuss what is negotiable and nonnegotiable. (Negotiable is a preference, and nonnegotiable is a requirement.)

Stuart's example:
Senior Financial Position Available

Small nonprofit company located in the suburbs seeks executive with twelve years experience in finance and accounting. Candidate must have an MBA in finance and knowledge of accounting and investing. Salary: $80,000, negotiable.

CRISIS-PROOFERS KNOW WHAT THEY WANT!

I ask my clients to do these exercises because it helps them to become aware of what they want, rather than simply taking what they can get. Your answers to the questions in this chapter should serve to give you a picture of how vulnerable you are to endangerment based on the external factors of your current job situation. Keep your answers together in your notebook.

As you look back over your answers to these assessments, you will probably be surprised at what you find. If you're like the majority of my clients, you will learn some information about yourself you never knew before.

Put your answers aside for now, but keep them handy. We will return to them in chapter 6. In the next chapter we will continue the assessment of your current situation, with the emphasis on the *internal* factors affecting your career: job burnout, stress, and finding your bliss.

## CHAPTER 3

CRITICAL CAREER QUESTIONS THAT LEAD TO BURNOUT OR BLISS

WHEN CRISIS IS THE CURRICULUM

On her thirtieth birthday, Susan made a collect call to her mother and started an argument. Susan was angry because she needed answers about life that her mother hadn't provided. Her mother listened patiently and then said, "Dear, you're not a car. When you were born, you didn't come with an operating manual."

Susan's feelings are understandable. In high school and college she set clear academic goals and worked hard to fulfill them. She sailed through graduate school and earned the advanced degree she needed to begin her career in business. Her first years as assistant brand manager were exciting, but soon the excitement wore off. She was ready for a change, but what? Susan found herself faced with challenges for which she felt unprepared.

Being an adult is difficult, and most of us approach it kicking, screaming, and blaming, like Susan. We grew up believing life should be easier. We want to know how to get the results we want and expect. We look for the one all-purpose solution we can use again and again. Instead, we find that nothing stays the same. What worked for us yesterday won't work today.

Our lives are a series of transitions, small and large. If we expect everything to go smoothly, we may find these transitions particularly confusing and painful. Yet when we choose to see that transitions are not terrible tragedies but inevitable, even predictable facts of life, our perspective changes in a significant way. We realize that we can develop within ourselves the resources needed to weather the changes and turn them to our advantage. We come a step closer to achieving what we want in our lives and becoming the masters of our fates.

Career issues and personal issues are interrelated. The fulfillment and satisfaction—or frustration and stress—we experience in one spill over into the other. I know of no better way to find happiness in life than through discovering and engaging in one's life work. Through our work we derive identity, belonging, recognition, and an overall sense that our lives are worthwhile. When our work springs from our interests, curiosity, and passion, it becomes an essential part of who we are.

This is evident in people who truly love their work. These lucky people seem to grow younger as they age and to be at peace with themselves. My neighbor Hal, for example, is a retired contractor. While helping me fix the electrical wiring on my deck one Saturday, he told me how his work had broadened him and helped him create significant friendships throughout his life. Another neighbor, Nancy, is a Montessori teacher with the openness of a young child. In a community of working parents, she is like a wise and loving grand-mother; children and parents alike are enraptured by her.

For people such as Hal and Nancy, their work is a way to interact with the world. It reflects who they are. Unfortunately, most of us do not find this level of satisfaction in our careers. When our job becomes stressful or provides too little or too much stimulation, when it is uninteresting or too demanding, it quickly becomes distasteful. Worse, it can affect our mental, emotional, and physical well-being.

In the last chapter we examined where you fit in the job market, your level of endangerment with respect to the type of work you do and the industry you work in, what factors are critical to job satisfaction, and how your personality fits in the marketplace. In this chapter, we examine where your chosen career fits in the larger scheme of your life, how it reflects your personal identity, your values, your priorities—how well it matches what you truly want. We will explore some of the ways in which people become endangered as a result of the choices they make—or fail to make. In considering important career questions, I will show you that certain career issues take on different meanings at different times in your life and why you must reevaluate your choices periodically to keep pace with the important changes in who you are.

I will then give you a number of tools to use in this reevaluation. *The Complete Job Burnout Scale* will assess your present level of job burnout—a prime source of endangerment—and *The Satisfaction Indicator* will let you see the level of satisfaction you are experiencing in various aspects of your life. In *The Values Indicator* we will look at the values you hold and whether they are in sync with your daily life. Finally, in the *Find Your Bliss Guide*, you will begin to identify some important pieces necessary for personal fulfillment in your life. All of this material will comprise the building materials for your crisis-proof career.

OUR CHANGING SELVES

Rod grew up in the ghettos of Trenton, New Jersey. Through education and training he became a disc jockey on a Philadelphia radio station. In his twenties, he loved his work, identifying strongly with his glamorous occupation. In the first couple of years he put a lot of effort into learning the business and mastering the difficult tasks. By the time he reached his early thirties he felt competent in the radio business. Over the years he saw countless radio people come and go, and he began to sense that he was cut from a different cloth. He didn't like having to be so thick-skinned to survive in the business. The glamour wore off and the trade-offs no longer seemed worth the price. The beliefs and values that had worked for him in his twenties simply felt empty to him now. Slowly, over a six-month period, he began to feel like a ship without a rudder, adrift.

Over the course of our lives we change, and what we need and want from our careers changes also. We must stay current with these internal needs and wants or risk endangerment, as Rod did. Knowing what questions to ask of ourselves is crucial. In my work with clients over the years, I have identified four recurring career questions.

Who Am I? Looking through old photo albums, we find pictures of ourselves at different ages. As we turn the pages, we might say, "Oh, yes, this is a photo of me at the beach when I was eight...Here I'm at college; I was such a serious student then...And here I am at twenty-five, just married."

We grow and change, but our need for a personal identity remains. When we have an identity to present to the world, we feel grounded. As a young man, Rod found a positive identity in radio. He had come a long way from the tough environment of his childhood. A decade later, however, he was a different individual. His early satisfaction had worn off, to be replaced by a sense of isolation as his perspective on life changed with maturity. What suited him in his twenties became unacceptable in his thirties.

Asking "Who am I?" raises personal issues that address where we truly fit in the scheme of things. If we don't come to terms with these personal issues, we become alienated and isolated.

What Are My Skills, Gifts, and Talents? This question addresses our competence and capacity to cope and prove ourselves in the world. These may be skills we learned through education or on-the-job training, gifts we were born with, or talents we have developed through special effort. Competence means the ability to hold a job, to be self-sufficient, to gain mastery, and to achieve something substantial. When we can't demonstrate competence, we feel weak and unable to cope.

Identifying our skills, gifts, and talents can become a complex task because the skills that others value in us may not be the ones we value. We may feel incompetent and unable to obtain a sense of mastery over our jobs, not because we lack the skills but because of the way they need to be done. In other situations, we may not be interested in practicing certain skills or may feel trapped in a role that forces us to use them in a limited way. Then we may feel competent but uninspired.

Marianne had an excellent facility for numbers and throughout her training was encouraged to become an accountant. At twenty-eight, she was on her way to becoming a CPA, and she had just a few more exams to pass, but she wasn't happy. Marianne discovered after several years of working at this first "real job" that she had little interest in the numbers and figures at which she was so adept. She enjoyed counseling people, not working with calculators and spreadsheets. A friend encouraged Marianne to gain some experience by working for a management consulting firm, where she could leverage her numerical skills with advising clients. Marianne soon found her expertise an effective way to bring her into contact with many interesting and creative people. Using the same talents she needed as a CPA, and by shifting the work setting slightly, Marianne had found a way to employ her talents that gave her personal satisfaction.

Where Do I Want to Make (or Continue to Make) a Contribution? The question of where we make our contribution refers to the context, setting, or environment in which we work. What do we need in terms of environment, company mission and goal, responsibilities, career advancement possibilities, relationship with a boss? These are some of the factors we examined in chapter 2 in the Critical Job Factors Assessment. Now we need to ask these questions in a larger, more personal context, in a way that will address our deeper needs and values: "Given my identity, where will I feel most valued? Where will I feel able to influence people and make my mark in a way that will have meaning?"

Choosing the right environment is key to feeling valued. If we try to make our contribution in the wrong context, we find our efforts undervalued and thwarted; we are left feeling underutilized. Rod came to feel alienated from the radio business; he no longer fit in and so felt isolated from his coworkers.

"You can make a difference" was a catchphrase in the 1970s that touched people's need to feel significant. When we feel significant, we feel important in the work we do, and people pay attention to us. We are recognized and taken into account.

What Trade-offs Must I Make? When we know who we are, know our skills and where we want to use them, we can assess the trade-offs involved in choosing any course of action. Every choice has a trade-off because every time we say yes to one thing, we say no to something else. The notion that you can simultaneously have it all is an illusion. Choices, sacrifices, and trade-offs are realities of life.

One Monday, Shaun received devastating news. The firm he worked for was moving from San Francisco to Detroit. Shaun had been treasurer of the alternative energy company for only one year. Prior to that, he had been unemployed for ten months during an extensive job search through which he landed his present job. Shaun couldn't bear the thought of being out of work again. He had his wife and two children to think of. On the other hand, he didn't want to move to Michigan. He and his family loved California.

To make the decision, Shaun and his wife took a trip to Detroit, and the contrast became more real. They realized then that living in California was very important to the family. Their parents lived there, and they loved the climate and the entire lifestyle they had built there. Shaun chose to stay in California.

When considering the trade-offs, you need to look at the risks involved in your choices. Shaun risked another extended period of unemployment, but weighing the options, he felt it was an acceptable trade-off. He counted on his experience in banking and utilities to see him through.

When we weather career and life transitions well, we feel competent and in control. When we don't, we feel out of control and may have a sense that we have failed. When you honestly weigh your options and accept trade-offs, you are deciding how to control the risks in your life, how to cope with transition, and how to avoid possible losses or tragedy. If we choose to take no risks and stay in our comfort zone, it may backfire in the end when we find what we want in life hopelessly out of reach. Failure to make transitions and take risks may result from many causes, some of which we will examine in the next chapter.

HOW THESE QUESTIONS AFFECT US AT DIFFERENT STAGES

In each decade of adulthood, you will have different answers to each of these four questions based upon your needs and the experiences that shaped you. Your answer to a question such as "Who am I?" will be different in your twenties than in your thirties. It's similar to climbing a spiral staircase. As you walk up the steps, the view keeps changing. So it is with these questions and your answers.

For people in their twenties, the identity question is the most important. Young men and women just starting out in life need a membership card to prove they "belong" in the adult world. Job titles provide a provisional answer to the identity question: "I am a management trainee for Macy's." Their job gives them a sense of place and security, at least for the time being. Along with this sense of identity arises a fear of not making it, of its being too different, or of closing off opportunities. Twenty-year-olds don't know what their gifts and skills are, so they venture out into the world to test themselves—sometimes cautiously and sometimes recklessly. An eighteen-year-old niece of mine told me the other day that she plans to be a rock star. Why not? This is a time to test many different environments and get feedback as to whether or not they fit. For a twenty-year-old, there are few trade-offs because they have nothing to lose except their innocence. There will be time for my niece to develop her fallback plan over the next few years.

My other niece took the job at Macy's, where she was thrown into a world of creative people. She learned how to select and price merchandise. Soon she became an assistant buyer. She got a car; she got a credit card. She got her own apartment and a live-in boyfriend. When she turned thirty a few years ago, she told me she had learned a lot in her twenties about having fun and how to handle herself in the grown-up world. Now she was ready to turn her attention to more serious things.

By their thirties, people worry less about membership and more about the quality of the role they play. They want to feel unique and special in their careers. This is usually the time to try out some more sophisticated roles, perhaps to go back to school for an advanced degree. After years of shifting around, there is a deepening of commitment to work and family. My niece married her boyfriend, became a mother, and received a promotion. Her role expanded and her responsibilities increased. At this time in her life, my niece, like others her age, has a better sense of her talents, skills, and gifts and wants to use them to distinguish herself personally and professionally.

In the trade-off department, "thirtysomethings" begin to distinguish fantasies from the realities. A friend of mine put it this way: "I'm coming to terms with my ordinariness." For some, there may be a conflict when they recognize that certain goals will not be reached. Toward the middle and end of their thirties, people begin to ask some philosophical questions about their lives: "Am I doing something that makes a difference in the world?" "Am I doing what I do because it is deeply satisfying for the long haul?"

By the end of the thirties, a person's identity is fairly well defined by his or her track record. Individuals may have been married and divorced, become single or vice president of marketing, but despite the changes they may have undergone, they have been labeled by family, friends, and colleagues. Most people will have acquired many possessions, so any moves they make will tend to be cautious and premeditated.

At forty, people are now making cautious and focused career decisions regarding the advancement or the leveling off of their careers. The question of where they want to make a contribution takes on special meaning because they may fear that they are losing their drive, or that they will be replaced by a younger coworker. They may fear appearing foolish trying out new things. For others this stage of life is marked by a courageous commitment to pursue new ventures, change jobs, or pursue second careers. Some may look for ways to consolidate efforts in an attempt to get rich quick. Or they may want to retreat from the competitive work world and create a more balanced life. One financially successful businessman in his late forties told me his heart attack changed his priorities very quickly. "I am having a very heady experience of being alive, and I don't want to jump back into my old life. It was a rat race."

Before people at this stage make any trade-offs, they look at potential losses and gains very carefully. For some people, this may be a time of great creativity. One colleague left her job and started her own business. "This is my last chance," she told me.

In their fifties, people have chosen their role in life and lived it.

They may wonder if they have used their time and talents well. They may regret not doing a number of things earlier in life or be concerned about having too little time in the future to catch up. They must make their contribution now in a clear, focused way. Some people do their best and most creative work now. They may have a sense of urgency: time is running out. As a result, they may be even more concerned with trade-offs.

This is a time for retrospection and analysis about the roles they played, the talents they used, the settings they chose, and the trade-offs they made along the way. They may evaluate the past with an eye toward integrating personal, family, and work lives. They want to think well of themselves, but may ask, "Have I made a contribution? Have I done enough?"

ANSWERING THE QUESTIONS FOR YOURSELF

To build your crisis-proof career, you will need to answer those four questions for yourself. To help you formulate your answers, we can break these larger questions into numerous smaller ones to allow you to examine each from several angles.

In your notebook, write down each of the following forty questions, one per sheet of paper. Then take your time and fill up the front and back of the page with your answers to each question. Forget about the quality of your responses—just get the ideas down. Put the critical part of you aside and forget about grammar, sentence structure, and syntax. Just write in a stream of consciousness whatever comes into your head. When inspiration flags, set the questions aside for a while, but keep them handy, writing on them as you can, over a period of several weeks.

Questions to Answer Under "Who Am I?"

1. What early ideas did I have about what I wanted to be when I grew up?
2. What messages did my mother give me (either verbally or through her behavior) about work?
3. What messages did my father give me (either verbally or through his behavior) about work?

4. What messages did my parents give me about learning and education?
5. What attributes and characteristics do I present to the world?
6. What attributes or characteristics would I like to develop?
7. Ten years from now, whom would I like to be?
8. If money and time were no object, what would I be doing?
9. At my retirement party, what do I want people to say about me?
10. How would a conversation go between the person I am and the person I want to become?

Questions to Answer Under "What Are My Skills, Gifts, and Talents?"

1. As a child, what talents did people reward me for?
2. As a child, when did others humiliate me about my performance?
3. What did others want me to be when I grew up?
4. If I were more honest about expressing my thoughts about my skills, gifts, and talents, what would I say?
5. What experiences do I want to have before I die?
6. What talents would I want to have developed?
7. What gifts come naturally?
8. What skills do I want to develop?
9. What skills have always been difficult?
10. If I had one wish and could be anything I want, what would it be?

Questions to Answer Under "Where Do I Want to Make (or Continue to Make) a Contribution?"

1. What is my definition of success?
2. What are the joys of my current situation?
3. What are the drawbacks of my current situation?
4. What would the ideal setting and job look like?
5. What would my ideal day look like?
6. If I were to name my deepest wants, what would they be?
7. When I think that I am going to die someday, what comes to mind?
8. Whom do I admire most in my family and why?

9. Who is the one person I admire and who I think has made an important contribution to the world?
10. What values do I hold most highly?

Questions to Answer Under "What Trade-offs Must I Make?"

1. What people were my role models as I was growing up?
2. What people did I learn negative lessons from growing up?
3. What qualities of experience am I seeking?
4. What was my former definition of success?
5. What am I most frightened to lose?
6. Next year at this time, what goals do I want to have accomplished?
7. Whom do I admire (or envy) and why?
8. What are the five worst things that can happen to me?
9. If I were willing to be more honest about my needs and wants, what would they be?
10. If I were willing to be more honest about expressing my emotions, what would I say?

How to Evaluate Your Answers

After you have written your answers to each question, put the notebook away for a week or two. Then, when you return to it, take the approach of a private detective with a mystery to solve. You are looking for clues, some common patterns to help you understand what is genuinely important to you. Read your answers in the spirit of a loving friend, not a cranky, frustrated career seeker.

After you have reread your entries, answer the following questions on another page in the notebook.

1. What are some common threads or patterns that emerge again and again?
2. What would the world be like if I were to have it "my way?"
3. What is keeping me from having it my way?

If you like, show your notebook to a friend or confidant and ask them to read your answers to the first series of questions. Then ask them to answer these last three questions about you on the basis of what they read.

Remember that there are no right or wrong answers to any of these questions. You might even have different answers at different times to the same question. We are flexible, changeable beings. Don't be afraid to give your most honest answers. Throughout this book there are other exercises to help you gain more clarity about the answers to some of these thoughtful questions. Then, in chapter 6, you'll take out these pages again and use them to create your crisis-proof career plan.

IF THERE SEEMS TO BE A PROBLEM...

As you sit down to complete these assessment instruments or to pursue other activities in your job search, you might get "stuck." Sometimes massive efforts produce few results. You may realize that the feelings you are having are beyond the scope of your career and have invaded your personal life for a long time as well. If this happens to you, and you feel as if you're caught, realize that you can get help.

Steven can't decide what he wants to be. At twenty this was permissible, but at thirty-eight Steven's time to develop a satisfying career is running out. He hates being a lawyer, but going back to school to retrain would take an enormous chunk of time to which he can't commit. So he stays where he is and complains, month after month. Meanwhile, Jean, after working for six years as a hospital nurse, stays put even though she hates her job because she's immobilized by the fear of leaving.

We all know people like this. Their lack of focus, commitment, and trust bind them to careers that sap them of their vitality. Even in less extreme situations, career issues may raise difficult personal issues. Most often the cause is the individual's self-esteem: How significant do I feel? How competent do I feel? How likable do I feel?

You should seek professional intervention (such as psychotherapy) anytime you become entrenched in a personal issue that is so intense or of such long duration that it affects your career. For example, even though Amy knows what she wants, she can't pick up the telephone and call people on her network list. This fear persists despite all her efforts to overcome it. Joe often tells the story about the time he was fired. Although it happened a decade ago, he describes it as if it happened yesterday. Joe's emotions about the incident are still so strong they may be keeping him from moving forward.

Whenever you feel that you don't have the resources to resolve an issue, it is important to consult with a professional who can help you sort out many issues ranging from burnout and being immobilized to massive anxiety. You don't have to be on the verge of a nervous breakdown to ask for help. A few short sessions may help you get unwedged.

LOSING GROUND: JOB BURNOUT

One consequence of failing to stay current with your career wants and needs is job burnout. Because it usually comes on gradually, you may suffer from burnout without being aware of it. How can you tell when it's happened to you? Here are three signals:

Too Tired to Take Geritol. You have no energy. The commercial you see on television telling you to "Just do it" seems to be for younger folks. Even watching people exercise on television wears you out. You feel as if you are riding around in a car with no shock absorbers. Regardless of the amount of sleep you get, you feel that you don't have the resilience to weather life's surprises. At the same time, life feels mechanical. You have to look at your schedule to know where you are. "It's eight o'clock on Monday morning, I must be in a staff meeting at work."

Everyone Has Gone to the Moon. You feel alienated, alone in a crowd. All your apprehensions and self-doubts surface, and you feel very negative, isolated, and resentful toward other people. You no longer feel that sense of well-being, that you are part of the life process. You feel you are performing on the high wire without a safety net under you.

How Did I Get Here? You don't feel connected to your accomplishments. You forget that you've achieved a lot in your life because right now none of it means anything. A friend of mine confided that she didn't feel she was getting anywhere but was just treading water, hardly keeping up with day-to-day demands. Yet in the last ten years, she had put two children through college, gone back to school at night to get her MBA, survived two mergers, and still landed on her feet.

Job burnout has many causes. Some people simply outgrow their jobs. Or they may not be in the right environment or using the right skills. The level of stimulation we receive in our jobs is also an important factor. Most people need the right balance of stimulation to feel good about themselves and what they do in their career. If you are understimulated, you may feel depressed and lethargic. For example, Penny described her two years in the Kalahari Desert while she served in the Peace Corps in Africa: "I felt as if I were living in slow motion. If one event happened that day, it was a big deal. There were no telephones, no fax machines. There was so little structure, so much free time to fill. I lived my life at a snail's pace. I thought I would love it and that Africa would be a great adventure. But I hated it." If you find that there is too little stimulation in your current situation, become curious. Look for what piques your interest or presents a challenge. The best way I know of to find your next best move is to complete the Find Your Bliss Grid later in this chapter.

Other people suffer from the opposite extreme: overstimulation. They put so much into their daily schedule, their lives zoom by faster and faster each year. When I asked a marketing-executive client of mine when he had time for himself, he laughed. "Every moment is filled. I never have any time alone, except for those rare moments traveling on a plane or in the bathroom or the shower. I asked my wife the other day, 'If this is success, how come I feel like a boiled chicken?'"

If you identify with this, take it as a cue to *slow down*. Look at your daily calendar and cut out some nonessential activities. Make regular dates with yourself to do nothing—and then keep them. Realize that you will get more from the activities you undertake if there are fewer of them.

THE COMPLETE JOB BURNOUT SCALE

Directions: If you are facing job burnout, here's a quiz to help you measure the severity of the problem. On a piece of notebook paper, write the numbers 1 through 16 to correspond to the following questions. Then indicate your answers to each question by a number from 0 to 5. Give yourself 0 if the area of your life is as good as ever or improved, and give yourself a 5 when that area has deteriorated badly.

1. Do you wear out more easily and feel as if you don't have much energy to bounce back? Do you wonder what happened to the energy of your youth?
2. Do you feel as if you don't look good lately, or are loved ones telling you something similar?
3. Are you working harder but feel as if you are producing less and less?
4. Are you feeling increasingly disillusioned and bitter?
5. Do you often feel tears behind your eyes, or a heaviness in your heart that you can't understand?
6. Are you forgetful of appointments, deadlines? Do you occasionally misplace personal possessions?
7. Are you increasingly irritable? More short-tempered? More disappointed in the people around you?
8. Is it an effort to see close friends and family members?
9. Are you too busy to do even routine things like make phone calls or read reports or send out your Christmas cards?
10. Are you suffering from minor physical ailments that you can't shake?
11. Do you feel disoriented when the activities of the day come to a halt?
12. Is joy something you read about or see on television commercials, but is not yours for the asking?
13. Are you thin-skinned when people joke about your foibles?
14. Does sex not seem worth the effort?
15. Do you find it hard to make small talk and appear friendly?
16. Are you having doubts about yourself and your abilities? Are you losing confidence in yourself?

Now add up your score. If your score is 0–30, you're doing fine. You are creating the right balance of stimulation and relaxation in your life. Try to become aware of how you do this, so you can keep a healthy balance that suits you. If your score is 31–50 you ought to be paying attention to what seems to be getting out of kilter. Build in more of what you are missing. At 51–79 you are over the edge of good mental health. It is time to do something. At 80 your stress level is in red alert. Do something now!

If your score is 30 or over, there is a lot you can do. First recognize the symptoms of job burnout and do something about their cause. Begin by putting some distance between yourself and your job. If you can't take a physical vacation, then you need to take a mental vacation. I remember that in my twenties if I didn't like a situation, I would leave—literally. Over the years, however, I discovered that I can "leave" without going anywhere. I simply sit in my swivel chair and change my attitude. On a sheet of notebook paper, under the heading "Complete Job Burnout Scale," list the areas in your life that have deteriorated and what strategies you can implement to counteract them, and those areas that have improved.

Our attitudes about ourselves, our job, and the world around us have a lot to do with how they affect us. If you find yourself wound up in your job, here are some suggestions that will help you get started with attitudinal reframing.

HOW TO STAY HUMAN ON THE JOB

1. Take small breaks and use the time to nourish yourself. Make a list of things that absorb you and make you forget time. Do what you like. Do things that bring you joy.

When the stress at work becomes too outrageous, Wayne puts on his sneakers and walks around the block. He comes back refreshed and ready to start again.

2. Relish these small refueling techniques with awareness. It is not the activity alone, but the quality of attention we bring to the activity. Any activity of our daily life, approached with the intention of developing concentration and clarity, can become a meditation.

Janet hated her hour-long drive to work and decided to do something about it. Before, she would deal with her impatience by finding as many distractions as possible, constantly pushing the buttons on the radio. Instead, she decided to sit in silence and feel her impatience and frustration during the inevitable gridlock on the way to work. Slowly, she worked to transform this feeling from frustration to acceptance. Over time she began to appreciate the time to plan her day.

3. Develop relationships in which you can be yourself on the job and off, so you don't have to go to work feeling like an impostor. Do

this by expressing your feelings. Giving each other permission to talk about feelings develops true camaraderie in the workplace.

During a three-hour delay at the airport on a business trip to Houston, coworkers Henry and Carl began to relax and discuss their impressions of their jobs, their coworkers, and each other. As a result, a bond was formed and they began to meet one evening a week on the way home to decompress and talk in strict confidentiality about their impressions of what was happening at the office.

4. Attempt to be present for yourself and others, and do fully and with involvement what presents itself next.

Claire knew that if she told Jake that he was in the doghouse at work, she might risk her standing with their boss. However, Claire valued Jake and his contribution to the organization. She would want someone to do the same for her if she was ever taken by surprise. She went ahead and took the risk. As a result, Jake was able to salvage his job, and his standing with their boss. Jake and Claire's friendship deepened. Claire was glad she didn't let Jake twist in the wind.

5. Ask yourself, "What is important? What is my own inner definition of success? Mine, not someone else's." Comparing yourself with someone else is silent sabotage. You need to realize that the answers don't exist *out there*. Listen to yourself telling your truth, even if it is out of step with the crowd. Inspiration is not a group activity.

At first Bob was delighted to be promoted to vice president of human resources. In this day of limited opportunities, he relished his move up the corporate ladder. Yet this feeling changed after a few months. The travel, the high-pressure tactics of his colleagues, and the new distance between himself and the rank and file quickly lost their charm. He began to long for the "good old days" when his time was more his own and he could interact with coworkers on a more casual basis. Before long, he applied for and received a transfer—back down the corporate ladder to his old position as manager. His colleagues thought he was crazy; his associates couldn't understand it. Bob, however, felt great about it.

6. Create a vision for yourself about how you'd like to be at work. Ask "Who am I at work? How do I really want to be?" Create some positive affirmations and work toward being that person.

Ann decided that she would like to be seen as the expert in her field. She wanted to stop feeling so frightened about losing her job. She assessed the situation and recognized an old pattern of hers was to try constantly to prove herself to people, even when they were already convinced. She decided to act the part of a competent authority. At the next staff meeting, Ann made her presentation. She had hardly sat down when an eager younger worker launched an attack against her idea. Ann would normally have been quick with a counterattack, but today she sat quietly. Sure enough, three other staff members came to Ann's defense and supported her idea. Ann began to feel like the person she had always wanted to be.

7. See the problem from others' point of view. This will help you anticipate the consequences of your actions and reassess the situation. It may be they have an insight to offer, if you take the time to look again.

Alison was told by her boss that she always seemed to want to do the project her way and that she consistently had a hard time taking direction. Alison's initial response was to resist her boss's evaluation. Upon second thought, Alison began to view this encounter as a test of her ability to subordinate her ideas and support her boss. She wondered how it would feel to do what her boss wanted and not resist. Then she realized that she had never done anything even approaching this her whole life. Although it was distasteful at first, Alison chose to view it as an experience in learning more about herself and her need to control things. After some months of effort, Alison mastered this new behavior and found it gave her greater flexibility in her relationships at work.

8. Make a friend of yourself. Keep a journal and write in it every day. How else can you know what you are thinking? Develop a sense of unlonely aloneness, learning to be by yourself.

Mike decided that each day he would spend an hour by himself before he met with his family for dinner. In that hour's time, he would sit down and write in his journal. It gave him the chance to unwind, reflect, and feel himself again after a long hard day. Through this exercise, he began to learn what he really needed and wanted in his life and career.

9. Develop your sense of humor and learn to play and laugh during the down times.

Sharon learned that some of the worst tension at work could be diffused if she kept a sense of humor and shared it with the other members of her work group. They soon learned to value this ability in Sharon and to practice it themselves.

10. Set realistic expectations. Make only reasonable agreements with yourself and then keep your agreements. Cultivate an appreciation of what you accomplish and forgive yourself for what you didn't do. Let go of the guilt.

11. Develop courage. It is an antidote against fear. You will succeed if you are fearless of failure. Think of fear as energy, just as gasoline fuels your car. Fear is the flip side of excitement. Fear can fuel you, if you choose to turn it into productive energy.

Chris was terrified when he began his new job. He wanted to do well and stay on for a long time. He felt that he needed to adapt to the new environment, keep a low profile, and not make waves. Then he saw how his coworkers were being intimidated by his boss. The man was using strong-arm tactics that Chris felt were inappropriate. He realized that he had to put aside his fear of losing his job and speak up honestly about his feelings. Chris was very direct when he gave his boss his feedback. To Chris's amazement, his boss listened. He told Chris he respected a person who could speak up and face off with him. His boss took his feedback and began to soften his style. Chris and his boss started on the right foot after all.

12. Learn to trust in what you love to do, continue to do it, and trust that it will take you where you want to go.

THE BIG PICTURE

Job burnout may be one indication that you need to make some changes in your life, but just where to make them may be difficult to know. Caught up in our daily routines, we often can't see where we stand in terms of our lives overall. Each of the following assessments is designed to give you that larger perspective. If you complete these exercises, you may be surprised to find your perspective rapidly takes a change for the better.

We'll begin with The Satisfaction Indicator, which helps you think about your personal levels of satisfaction in a variety of contexts. It can identify what is most meaningful to you now as well as what is no longer satisfying. It can tell you if you need to make a change and what areas need improvement.

THE SATISFACTION INDICATOR

In the scale below first evaluate how satisfied you are with each of these areas in your life: 1 is low and 10 is high. Define each category any way that suits you. Circle the number that represents your level of satisfaction now.

1.	Your current job	1	2	3	4	5	6	7	8	9	10
2.	Your career advancement	1	2	3	4	5	6	7	8	9	10
3.	Your financial situation	1	2	3	4	5	6	7	8	9	10
4.	Your energy level	1	2	3	4	5	6	7	8	9	10
5.	Your friendships	1	2	3	4	5	6	7	8	9	10
6.	Your health	1	2	3	4	5	6	7	8	9	10
7.	Your physical self	1	2	3	4	5	6	7	8	9	10
8.	Your family	1	2	3	4	5	6	7	8	9	10
9.	Your spouse or life partner	1	2	3	4	5	6	7	8	9	10
10.	Your spiritual life	1	2	3	4	5	6	7	8	9	10
11.	Your creative self	1	2	3	4	5	6	7	8	9	10

Look at the differences for each category between where you put yourself and the highest score of 10.

Write down in your notebook the answers to these questions:
1. What would it take to raise all my scores to 10?
2. What are the obstacles keeping me from being a 10 in each category?
3. What would I need to do to take action or change my attitude to be a 10 in every category?
4. Am I willing to do these things?
5. Why not?

As before, keep your answers handy so you can return to them later.

THE VALUES INDICATOR

Beyond the day-to-day routine is the larger question of what matters to us in life. When our values are incongruent with the setting in which we work and live, we may lose interest or feel out of touch. On the other hand, when our values are reflected in our environment, it adds another level to the richness and meaning of life.

First, rate each of the twenty-eight values in the column below as low (no value to you), moderate (has some value to you), or high (most important, nonnegotiable). Second, take the ones you rated high and on a separate sheet of notebook paper rank these in numerical order according to importance, 1 being the most important value to you. Third, ask yourself if the top five values are being expressed in your current situation and write a sentence on how each value is put into action or behaviors in your life.

Rachel ranked her top values in descending order: creativity, wealth, and freedom. Having done this, it was immediately apparent to her that her job as a computer programmer for an insurance company did not reflect these core values. It helped her realize why she was dissatisfied with her job.

VALUE	LOW/MODERATE/HIGH
1. Achievement (a sense of accomplishment, mastery)	
2. Advancement (promotions)	
3. Adventure (new and challenging experiences)	
4. Affection (love, caring)	
5. Competitiveness (winning, taking risks)	
6. Cooperation (working well with others, teamwork)	
7. Creativity (being imaginative, innovative)	
8. Economic security (having savings, feeling financially safe)	
9. Fame (being well-known, celebrated)	

10. Family happiness
    (harmony, a sense of security)
11. Freedom
    (independence, autonomy)
12. Friendship
    (close relationships with others)
13. Health
    (physical well-being and freedom from
    illness)
14. Helpfulness
    (assisting others, improving society)
15. Inner Harmony
    (being at peace with oneself)
16. Integrity
    (honesty, sincerity, standing up for
    beliefs)
17. Involvement
    (participating with others, belonging)
18. Loyalty
    (duty, respectfulness, obedience)
19. Order
    (tranquillity, stability, conformity)
20. Personal Development
    (use of potential)
21. Pleasure
    (fun, laughs, a leisurely lifestyle)
22. Power
    (control, authority, or influence over
    others)
23. Recognition
    (respect from others, status)
24. Religion
    (strong religious beliefs, closeness to
    God)
25. Responsibility
    (accountability for results)

26. Self-respect
     (pride, sense of personal identity)
27. Wealth
     (making money, getting rich)
28. Wisdom
     (understanding life, discovering
       knowledge)

Summing Up Your Values

On a piece of notebook paper under the heading "The Values Indicator," answer the following questions: What are the values you ranked most highly? What are your top five values? Are these values expressed in your current job? If not, what are the values of your current situation?

If you like, show your list to a friend. Ask him or her if your behavior demonstrates that these indeed are your top values, or if it seems to indicate some quite different values.

THE CAREER AS A MIRROR

The career journey is a mirror of your relationship with yourself. It is an ongoing process that requires time, truth, incubation, periods of barrenness, brilliant flashes, and long, steady effort. When you are equipped to recognize the patterns, it relieves your anxiety about the unknowable aspects of the future. You can move more easily from transition to transition, opening more fully to the hide-and-seek nature of the self.

On the basis of the previous assessments, and in other perhaps less tangible ways, you may realize that you need something different in your life. But what?

Keith Thompson, a guest at Joseph Campbell's eightieth birthday party, told of an incident about this teacher, writer, and foremost authority on myths. A young man stepped out of the celebrating crowd to ask Dr. Campbell, "How is a person to go about finding his or her myth?"

"Where is your deepest bliss?" Joseph responded.

"I don't know. I'm not sure."

"*Find* it," he sang back, "and then *follow* it."

FIND YOUR BLISS GRID

Bliss is not all-engulfing ecstasy. Bliss starts small and overtakes us gradually. The purpose of this exercise is to enable you to identify the small things that will lead you to your bliss and those things that keep you from it. Finding your bliss involves knowing what you like and dislike to do, what gives you satisfaction and reflects your core values. It will tell what you want to do again and what you hope never to have to do again in your personal and professional life.

Directions: Take a piece of notebook paper and fold it in half. Fold it in half again. Now unfold it and you have four boxes. Number these boxes 1 to 4 and write one of the following headings in each.

Box #1 *Things that I never want to do again.*

These are things you have done, and perhaps have done well, and could always do again but hope you won't have to. Examples of this are write expense reports, do a budget, report to a boss who is a slave driver, spend another winter in Chicago, wear a tie to work, commute two hours every day, have an office with no windows, wear a hat and wing-tip shoes, stand at attention, meet unrealistic deadlines, sell a product you don't believe in, manage poor performers.

Box #2 *Things people say I do well, but I take for granted.*

These are things you've done before but feel are routine and uneventful. Examples: grasping the big picture, problem-solving, dressing well, being organized, mentoring people, leading staff meetings, forecasting economic trends.

Box #3 *Things I like to do and wouldn't mind doing again.*

These are small, simple activities that you enjoy. Examples: journal writing, playing music, helping people, gardening, remodeling the house, closing sales, taking seminars, listening to interesting speakers, talking to strangers on the plane, helping your spouse solve a personal problem, taking the kids to outings, going to the movies.

Box #4 *Things I'd like to learn more about if I had the time, money, and other resources.*

These may be practical or impractical. Examples: new computer software, developing a new marketing niche, playing the piano, deer-proof and drought-resistant gardening, family genealogies, hooking up your computer to your electronic piano, doing a time-and-motion study for your department, learning to dance the lambada.

Your entries under headings 1 and 2 deal with your basic skills, your "comfort zone." These are things that have given you experience and activities that have always gotten you work, but are unchallenging to you, perhaps even boring and repetitive. Boxes 3 and 4 deal with a stretch, a risk, a challenge. They are the edge of your growth. This is where your bliss lies—in areas you enjoy, areas you are curious about both personally and professionally.

If you have difficulty completing this exercise, you may be confusing stating your preferences with making decisions. This may be a result of your desire not to make commitments—one of the demons discussed in chapter 4.

The Next Step: As you write your answers on the grid (remember, the more the better), patterns will become apparent. When you have finished, take a few minutes to look over your answers for more patterns, highlighting them for future reference.

We will work more with your answers on this grid in chapter 5, "Expanding the Horizons" and chapter 6, "Living by Your Own Agenda." For the present, put this grid in your notebook.

THE FABRIC OF OUR LIVES

There are no guarantees. Tragedy and loss are as much a part of life as achievement, happiness, and success. How do we prepare ourselves to face these inevitable challenges and transitions? The best that we can do is to develop within ourselves the tools we need to relieve the terror and uncertainty life changes bring. I believe we accomplish this by thinking of life as a learning laboratory. When we frame major events as lessons, we stop reacting to transitions by asking "Why me? Why now?" Instead we ask," What lesson can I learn from this? What purpose can this difficult circumstance serve in my life?"

Bill Moyers interviewed Laurence Olivier before he died. He asked Olivier if he had ever experienced stage fright. Olivier said he threw up backstage before every performance. The astonished Moyers shot back, "What did you do?" Olivier replied, "I learned how to work with it."

When we learn who we truly are, we, like Olivier, can learn to work with our gifts and limitations, choose the trade-offs and make the contributions we want. When we apply our self-knowledge to a crisis-proof career, it can serve as a road map, as a set of actions to take when we lose our job or face important transitions. We can take steps to change the terror into creative energy and find our way.

In the next chapter we'll look at some of the forms of self-endangerment, which I call the demons within, that may be keeping you from working at your best.

## CHAPTER 4

THE DEMONS WITHIN

SELF-IMPOSED BARRIERS TO SUCCESS

Dick Connell sat in my office staring blankly at the business plan spread out on the table between us. "Finding money is hard," he said flatly. "No one wants to fund a business like mine, so why bother?" He shrugged. "I guess I just don't have what it takes."

Dick had spent weeks developing a business plan for his restaurant, a lifelong dream. He had planned for everything, and now it was time to find the backers who would make his dream a reality. Yet here he was, stymied and hesitant. What went wrong?

"I don't have what it takes."

"You can never rest on your laurels. If you take your eye off the ball, you drop it."

"You've got to know what you want to do in life, and then stick with it."

"I'd like to start my own business, but I'm afraid I'd fail like my father."

I frequently hear these and other similar statements from my clients. At first they surprised me. They seemed to emerge out of nowhere. After weeks of productive work together on marketing strategies, assessment analysis, and job factors, our progress would come to a screeching halt.

Today I recognize these statements for what they are: signals that someone is clinging to old habits and ways of thinking that can hinder and downright sabotage his or her career. The fact is, there is more to crisis-proofing a career than just learning the simple skills of writing a resumé, networking, finding the right job, and negotiating an offer. You can do all of these and still never reach your goal. If you are just going through the motions but don't believe in your goals or in your ability to reach them, or if they are not your goals but someone else's, success will probably elude you, as it threatened to elude Dick.

I counsel many successful people. You might expect them to trust themselves and recognize their job search as a temporary state of affairs. After all, they have climbed many other mountains before this. Yet even the most successful people in the midst of a major transition can be plagued by self-doubts brought on by self-imposed barriers.

The most common forms of barriers are self-defeating thoughts, achievement addiction, belief gaps, and the fear of risk. While they may cause problems at any time in our lives, they are most likely to surface during transitions, when we are at our most vulnerable. They differ from other forms of endangerment in that they have nothing to do directly with how we interact with our jobs or the job market. I call these the *demons within* because they involve only our relationship with ourselves—our values, beliefs, and ways of thinking. The danger of these demons is that they can cause us to settle for less than we want in our careers and less than we could have, because we don't trust ourselves enough to strive for our heart's desire. They make the difference between sprinting to the finish line and never making it because we gave up along the way. These demons must be slayed before you can go on to complete your crisis-proof career.

The demons within are particularly insidious because they are usually unconscious habits and patterns we build into our lives without knowing it, so they can go undetected for years. What's more, each person has his or her own version of these barriers because they are a combination of many different habits; no two combinations are quite the same. This makes them harder to detect. When you can identify the demons operating in your life, and see them for what they are, you can find ways to overcome them.

CHANGING YOUR PERSPECTIVE

One of the most important survival skills we can learn to weather these changing times is to shift our perspective from an external orientation to an internal one. We must learn to trust ourselves for answers. We need to stop blaming and start taking responsibility for our life choices; we must summon the courage to confront ourselves about what we really want if only we could step outside of our comfort zone.

Our comfort zone is the place from which all transitions begin. It is the job we've held for a number of years that we now take for granted; it is the routine that keeps us on the treadmill. Here we use our proven skills, consolidate our talents, prove our competence. We know who we are and we feel safe and comfortable. Unfortunately, our tenure in any one comfort zone is necessarily limited. If we tarry too long, we become bored and soon suffer from job burnout and dissatisfaction. At other times some exterior event occurs—such as job loss—and we are forced out of our comfort zone.

Whether we leave our comfort zone as a result of internal or external pressures, the problem remains the same: How can we learn to use this time of transition to prepare ourselves to find inspired work and discover what we really want to do? I tell my clients that this transition is their chance to build a bridge out of the comfort zone toward their dreams. They can do this by taking small, manageable risks that will eventually enable them to create crisis-proof careers.

This is easier said than done, however. The demons within are waiting to emerge just at the point we need courage most. Here is how it happened to one client.

My contact at a bank called to tell me that she was sending over Theresa Tetsen, vice president and regional district manager of corporate banking. No one at the bank wanted Theresa to leave, but she had turned down the new job that was offered her after the restructuring of their division and asked for a severance and outplacement package instead.

When I had my first meeting with Theresa, she seemed relieved and elated. "I've worked in banking for eighteen years. My son is grown and out of the house, I am forty-five years old, and I am ready to try something new," she told me confidently.

The first several weeks we met extensively. We assessed her marketability, the settings she enjoyed working in, what she enjoyed doing, and things that she never wanted to do again. Theresa wanted to go back to school to get an undergraduate degree. Then she wanted to travel and work in different parts of the world. She had never been outside the United States. I gave her the names of three university faculty members who could evaluate her work experience. I told her about accredited college programs that could give her college credit based on her work experience. Another option she considered was to go back to school after she had traveled and worked for a year. I put her in touch with some travel and work-abroad programs as well as some clients who had done something similar the year before. She had the names and phone numbers in her hand when she left my office.

As it turned out, she never called any of them. Despite her desire for new vistas and challenges, when faced with the real possibility of moving into unknown territory, Theresa became immobilized with doubts. The next time I saw her, Theresa told me she had decided to remain in banking. As I gently questioned her, I could see the self-imposed barriers appearing. "Well, I really don't want to go back into banking, but it's the easiest thing to do and I know where I stand." Later she asked, "What made me think I could really change careers? You can't teach an old dog new tricks. I'll never succeed at anything outside of banking."

Theresa didn't want to take even the small risk of calling someone and discussing her situation. She feared appearing vulnerable or failing in a new endeavor. "What if I find I can't do it? What a waste of time!"

Let's take a closer look at Theresa's change of heart. She was experiencing the first demon: self-defeating thoughts.

THE FIRST DEMON: SELF-DEFEATING THOUGHTS

"I don't have what it takes."

As we look out on the world, we see a series of neutral, random events. It is our eyes and minds that interpret these events in a continuous sequence of thoughts, an internal dialogue. Your feelings, such as hope or fear, result from your thoughts, not the actual events, which in themselves are neutral. If you look out at the world and register self-defeating thoughts, you will see negative sights and feel negative feelings. Conversely, you can choose to view the world through self-enhancing thoughts, to see the same things and feel differently.

This is why self-defeating thoughts are so dangerous. Crisis-proofing begins with an assessment of your present situation and a vision of what you want in life. Self-defeating thoughts bias both the assessment and the vision and keep you from productively following your own agenda. To overcome these self-defeating thoughts, you must work on transforming them on a daily basis. I have identified ten basic patterns of thinking, although they appear in an endless variety of guises.

1. Black-and-white thinking. These are all-or-nothing thoughts about yourself such as, "I am always going to be unemployed," "I'll never find a good job," or "I'll have to work here forever." Notice how unhappy you feel when you hear yourself thinking these thoughts. When you have these thoughts, you are looking at the situation in finite categories.

You can frequently identify black-and-white thoughts by words such as *never, always, forever, nothing, ever,* or other words that are unprovisional and absolute. Most importantly, they are pessimistic and negative. For example, when Theresa said, "You can't teach an old dog new tricks" or "I'll never succeed at anything outside of banking," she was demonstrating black-and-white thinking.

In contrast, creative thinking is provisional and conditional, and generally optimistic. Life is not absolute, but full of shades of gray. Theresa has more than one option outside banking, and some options will prove a better fit than others. No one is a success or a failure at everything. Thinking that way leads to perfectionism.

Risk taking is not all-or-nothing. Although she may not have been ready to commit everything to her vision of a new life, Theresa could have found small, manageable risks that would get her started. Taking one or two credit classes at the local college, for example, would have given her an idea of what going back to school might entail. Planning shorter trips to foreign countries would demonstrate to her the pleasures and strains of traveling abroad.

2. "It will never change" thinking. You look at your situation as a never-ending pattern of defeat, striving, and failure. You overlook that people and situations change all the time. For example, Theresa felt, "I've been in banking eighteen years. I only have banking skills, nothing else," or "With my luck, wherever I go, they'll probably restructure, too." The characteristics of this thinking are generalizations. You take one incident and expand it to include your whole career.

In contrast, more accurate thinking might include, "What a bad break. Transitions are sometimes hard, but I can use this time to explore some of the dreams I've never had a chance to before."

3. The glass is half-empty. Looking at the situation, you see its negative and ignore its positive aspects. You don't look at what you have going for you, only what isn't going your way. After the demons set in, Theresa saw her only choice as returning to banking. She felt trapped. She wasn't looking at the advantages in her situation: a good severance package and the help of a personal outplacement counselor, both of which could help her to explore her many available options. The glass was really half-full.

4. "Nothing counts." You resign yourself to hopelessness and discount what you can do to change the situation. Fearful of taking a new risk, Theresa quickly fell back into resignation. "I've wasted eighteen years of my life and I still don't feel prepared. I'm not up to the challenge of starting a whole new life. What's the use? I might as well go back to what I know, even if I dislike it."

In contrast, she had the option of believing in herself and her ability to go forward in her life. She'd met many challenges before. She might have thought, "Here's my chance to change my life, my situation, and my destiny. It's up to me, but I can get help from others when I need it."

5. Catastrophizing in the future. You discover psychic powers and develop an ability to predict how events will turn out and how others will respond (usually not in your favor). Theresa told me, "I'll probably end up in banking and hate it," "I will never succeed in anything other than banking," and "Only bankers want me."

Here is where the self-fulfilling prophecy comes into play. In an effort to protect ourselves from disappointment, we prepare for the worst. The problem is that the worst is too often exactly what we get when we think this way. This thinking closes off the options that could prove us wrong. It undermines our efforts to bring about a different and positive outcome.

6. Exaggerating or minimizing. You take the smallest part of a conversation, interview, or situation and exaggerate it to represent how poorly everything went and downplay the other parts that went well. When Theresa told me, "People say it's really hard to change careers," I wondered exactly how many people she had talked to, one or ten? Did they all express the same opinion, or did she selectively hear only those opinions that came close to her worst thoughts?

Think of the difference between Theresa's statement and the following statements she may have heard, but altered to conform to her fears:

"It's hard to change careers, but once you put out the effort, it's worth it in the end."

"I've heard that it's hard to change careers if you don't know what you're doing."

"It's hard to change careers because most people don't have the time and money needed to make the transition."

7. "I feel therefore I am." You take the way you are feeling in the moment to prove that nothing good is going to happen. You reason with your emotions. Because things feel so bleak, you assume they really are. On the day Theresa talked to me, she was feeling particularly down. "What happens if I fail? Maybe I shouldn't try." She was taking her fear of failure as a reason for not trying. In fact, feelings are just a reflection of self-defeating thoughts. When you change the thoughts, you can change the feelings.

8. Musts, shoulds, oughts. You corral yourself into doing things that you don't want to do with a litany of musts, shoulds, and oughts. You flagellate the dutiful and responsible part of you that sets impossible standards for perfection. Theresa felt, "I should get a job in banking so it will look better on my resume" and "I ought to stay with what I know." Thinking this way pacified Theresa's conscience, even though it wouldn't make her happy in the long run.

9. Stick'ems. You label yourself by old standards and generalizations. This is an extreme form of "It'll never change" thinking. Theresa felt, "I've been in banking for eighteen years for a reason:

only bankers would consider me." Other statements such as, "I'm an old dog, I can't learn new tricks," "I don't have the education," "I've never been smart," and "I'm not good at that," are typical of the self-defeating labels people stick on themselves.

In truth, none of us can be equated with just one aspect of ourselves. We are complex, multifaceted, and ever changing. To label ourselves assumes that we are simplistic and static. What we have done in the past does not dictate what we can do in the future.

10. Blaming. You blame yourself for all the things that went wrong, not realizing that you are just a part of a larger picture. Or you blame other people and overlook ways in which you might have been part of the problem. Theresa blamed herself when she thought that she had wasted eighteen years of her life in banking, and she had nothing to show for it.

By now you might think that Theresa was the most resistant client in the world. Far from it. We all go through these thoughts to a greater or lesser degree when faced with the prospect of change in our lives. Career transitions especially activate self-defeating thoughts as we worry about our competence and ability to perform. This is true whether we decide to make a job change or we are asked to leave. Fortunately, there are ways to counteract your self-defeating thoughts.

Taming Your Self-Defeating Thoughts

The ways in which you perceive and think about yourself and your situation can halt your progress toward a crisis-proof career or speed you on your way. In his research on cognitive therapy and depressed patients, Dr. Aaron T. Beck found that a positive attitude makes a significant difference in the outcome of one's actions, that if your inner dialogue is more loving and trusting, you will more easily bring each situation to its successful conclusion. Charles Garfield, in his book *Peak Performers*, similarly suggests that if you can visualize a positive outcome and say self-assuring things to yourself, you greatly increase the chances of reaching your goal.

Here are some suggestions to turn around negative thinking.

Monitor your self-defeating thoughts. Take each thought and make it into an alternative, self-enhancing thought. For example,

Theresa might reassure herself, "I don't know yet what I am going to do, but I can give myself time to figure it out. It's important to allow myself to be in transition so I can find the best option."

Think of something a loved one might say to you to console you, or that you yourself would say to a close friend who came to you with the same problem, something compassionate and reassuring.

Identify self-defeating thoughts and reason with yourself. Play devil's advocate with those negative thoughts. For every negative thought you think, turn it around. Build a lawyer's case as to why the opposite is also true. Here logic, not compassion, prevails. Tell yourself some alternatives that also make sense.

Instead of thinking, "I've been in banking for eighteen years already, so I'd better stay," Theresa might just as reasonably say, "I've been in banking for eighteen years and I've gone as far as I want to there. It's time for something new." Or instead of using the argument "It is painful and difficult to be in transition; I'll just return to where I can feel safe," Theresa might just as well say, "It's going to be a little hard because it's something I haven't done before. That's exactly why it's worth doing it."

Keep a personal journal. When you realize that you are thinking sabotaging thoughts, write them in a section of your notebook, telling when, where, who, what, and how. Record the dialogues you are having. On one side of the page write your self-defeating thoughts. Then draw a line down the page. On the other side of the page write what a reassuring friend might say in response to each thought. Do this faithfully. This is one way of letting go of the thoughts and distancing yourself from them.

Confide in a friend. Take a loved one or friend into your confidence. Tell your friend about what you are doing and ask for his or her support. Build a team of people you can call and talk to or meet with, people who are available to listen to you talk about your transition.

Choose to stop thinking self-defeating thoughts. When they become too much, just say "Stop!" to yourself and start thinking about something else. Two conflicting thoughts cannot occupy the same space. I had a client who used to wake up at three A.M. and couldn't go back to sleep. All the unresolved conflicts of his day used to keep him awake. Finally, he thought of an idea. "I imagine my mind is like a big ocean, and during that time of night my mind is washing to shore the flotsam and jetsam of the day. I don't pay any attention to it."

Put yourself in the other person's shoes and have a dialogue. Instead of blaming yourself or others, see how it feels to look at other people's motives. You might gain a perspective you didn't have before. If you are feeling angry at your former boss, take a piece of paper and draw a line down the middle. On one side write out what you want to say uncensored. On the other side write out his/her responses uncensored. Write out the conversation between him/her and you as if you are writing a screenplay. Do this until you feel some change in the conversation or a shift in mood or understanding. Then tear it up and throw it away or put it in an envelope and stick it in a drawer to be opened a year from now. (Don't send it to your boss! You don't want to burn any bridges!)

Learn to laugh at yourself. Humor is another strategy to defuse your negative thinking. If you can find something funny in what's happening, it frees you up to take action and escape from the negativity. Imagine how you would feel if the situation were a skit on *Saturday Night Live* or a *New Yorker* cartoon. Get some humorous perspective.

Ted went home really beat one evening after a two-hour interview. When his wife asked him how he did, he replied, "Terrible!" In a moment, totally out of character, he began mimicking the interviewer's intimidating style. He got such relief out of doing this that he started exaggerating it for his wife. They both laughed harder and harder. Right then, Ted made a deal with himself that he was going to give vent to this healthy expression and not keep his frustrations in.

Find ways to relax and reward yourself. Find an activity that helps you take your mind off the current situation and reward yourself. Some of my clients choose gripping mysteries, trashy novels, long walks in the country, a bike ride, window-shopping, watching television, or a movie. Plan larger rewards when you have accomplished a certain goal.

Your mind is very powerful. It can work for you as well as against you. You are the only one who has control over it. You can choose self-defeating thoughts or self-enhancing thoughts. Crisis-proofers choose the latter.

THE SECOND DEMON: ACHIEVEMENT ADDICTION

"You can never rest on your laurels. If you take your eye off the ball, you drop it."

When Janet was a little girl, her parents wanted the best for her. They knew that competition would always be tough, and they wanted her to be prepared. Janet responded by trying to be the best in everything in order to make them happy. Eventually Janet measured herself by how much she achieved. She got into the right college, married the right man, had two children, and "I even chose the right career!" she joked. "My parents are long since gone, but I still thrive on this drive to achieve. It's the only thing that seems to keep me going at times. I look for a challenge and then try to master it. I just don't know how to direct my energy any other way."

In childhood, our parents represent the world to us. We want to please them and so we choose to follow their subtle cues about the way they want us to be. "Be smart and popular" was Toby's message. "Be a doctor and make us really proud of you" was Bernie's message. "Get married and get a teaching credential" was Susan's message— "You can always get a job as a teacher," her mother prophesied. Later our schools underscored our parents' message that mastery and performance gain approval and attention.

Trouble occurs when the achievement is emphasized at the expense of learning and planning. The positive nature of the message becomes skewed. Rather than being loved or recognized for who we are, we may come to believe that it is what we do, not who we are, that earns us love and respect. This can set up a lifelong pattern of ceaseless striving to be more, do more, and achieve more. Instead of being human beings, we become human doings. This is achievement addiction.

As adults, we continue to set goals and strive to reach them. Then, just as we come close to attaining them, we set the goals out further or find some way to make them harder. So we put ourselves in the familiar state of endless struggling for approval, just the way we did as children. In the end, we never permit ourselves the satisfaction of having met the goal because we are already busy with the next.

The compulsion to achieve begins so early in our lives that we may be unaware of its influence. We may allow it to take its toll on our relationships, on our perspective on life, even on our health. It can become so familiar, like an old friend, that we don't realize it causes us to work against ourselves or even that we have a choice not to repeat the pattern.

Achievement addicts' self-esteem is measured by what they have accomplished lately. Not surprisingly, their self-esteem fluctuates like the stock market. Bob is a salesman. If he hasn't closed a sale in a while, he feels like a failure. This measure of ability causes him to vacillate between depression and elation, unfulfillment and fulfillment, based on the tally of accomplishments that day. To live this way is tantamount to being on an emotional roller-coaster ride.

Achievement addicts are at a particular disadvantage during transitions. I have heard many a client, after looking for a job for two weeks, say, "If I am so good, how come I haven't found a job by now?" Achievement addiction renders the job seeker incapable of believing in him/herself long enough to develop a crisis-proof career plan, or long enough to create a vision of what is possible and to work to make the possibility a reality.

Are You An Achievement Addict? The Test

Are you an achievement addict, sabotaging your career with ceaseless striving? Below are twenty-five common statements by achievement addicts. Rate each one with a number from 0 to 3 corresponding to these four answers:

3 = To a great extent I feel this way.
2 = To a moderate extent I feel this way.
1 = To a lesser extent I feel this way.
0 = I don't feel this way at all.

1. If I'm to be a worthwhile person, I must be outstanding in at least one major aspect of my life.
2. I must be a useful, productive, creative person or life has no purpose.

3. I find it hard to take time for myself.
4. I think that people who are smart are more worthy than those who are not.
5. I don't measure up if I don't do as well as other people.
6. If I lose my job, then I am a failure as a person.
7. If I can't do something well, there is little point in doing it at all.
8. I don't like to display my weaknesses.
9. I'd rather do things myself than get help.
10. I get upset if I'm criticized.
11. If I don't set high enough standards for myself, I will end up being a second-rate person.
12. I'm always comparing myself to others.
13. I don't often feel very successful.
14. I feel more comfortable if I have a list of things to do.
15. It is important to me how a job will look on my resumé.
16. I can't take time off without worrying that I am missing something or how it looks to others.
17. I can't take my eye off the ball because I am afraid others will get ahead of me.
18. I feel better if I complete all the tasks on my list for that day.
19. If I am not doing something, I feel I am wasting time.
20. I could never take a nap during a weekday, unless I was really ill.
21. I get bored and restless when a goal is completed and no new challenge is in sight.
22. I set unrealistic deadlines for myself.
23. I hurry even when I have plenty of time.
24. I get impatient when someone is doing a job that I can do quicker.
25. I push to finish a task even when I am tired.

What Does Your Score Mean?

Tally the numbers you've used to respond to all the statements. The highest possible score is 75. The lowest possible score is 0. If you scored 0–25 you are enjoying getting to your goal. You probably select reasonable objectives and work productively to meet them. If you scored 26–50, you are probably going overboard with bouts of "workaholism." Become more aware of this tendency in yourself. If you scored above 50, you are one of the achievement addicts who do too much and get too little enjoyment out of it.

The Way Out

If you are an achievement addict, remember that it took a lifetime to get this way—it's going to take some time for you to recover. Here are some easy things to practice to decrease the pressure and sense of urgency on yourself, especially during your job search.

Remember that it is the process, not the result, that is important. You have the option to make this career transition a time to panic or a time to learn and deepen your relationship with yourself. In the long run your self-understanding will prove the more valuable. Jobs change, but you take yourself wherever you go.

This is a time to remember your Find Your Bliss Grid, where you listed areas you'd like to learn more about. Choose especially activities where you can expand your skills and broaden your outlook. Taking a class, for example, will enable you to meet new people and experience other facets of yourself.

Give yourself permission to live in a state of "I don't know" for a period of time—three months is optimum. Explore new possibilities and try on some new behaviors.

Patty made a list of all the books she wanted to read but never felt she had the time for. Systematically, she set aside one hour a night to read instead of watch television. George had trouble talking to people at parties. He decided that he would get more active in his church community and use this time to increase his network of new friends. He learned a lot about how to meet people comfortably and relieve the anxiety he had formerly felt.

This is a time to stretch out of your comfort zone, taking small, manageable risks that will reinforce your confidence to take on larger and larger risks. Learn new, enjoyable things even while you focus the bulk of your effort on your job search.

Cultivate patience and compassion for yourself. These are what achievement addicts lack. Become a friend to yourself. Think of someone in your past who accepted you openly and lovingly. To this person, it didn't matter what you did, only that you were yourself. Practice being that way with yourself.

First, write down some situations in which you normally feel impatient, perhaps at the checkout line in the supermarket or on the road behind a dawdling driver. Then, when you find yourself feeling impatient in those situations, stop and ask, "How can I think about this in a way I can cultivate patience and compassion?" Theresa told me that she found herself behind a slow-moving car on the highway, but instead of cursing and tailgating, she said to herself, "This person is keeping me from speeding and getting a ticket." She said she laughed out loud at her patience and subsequent good mood.

When Wayne's letter to a prospective employer was returned for insufficient postage, Wayne chose not to get angry or impatient with himself. Instead he reasoned, "This guy is probably inundated with resumés right now. Mine will come after the onslaught." Catch yourself and reorient your thinking toward patience.

Become aware of your impatience and your sense of urgency. Notice how anxiety propels you into action. Develop the ability to notice your impatience, detach from it, and refuse to take it seriously when you recognize its old patterns. Let the impatience and urgency pass, then see what lies underneath. Theresa found that under her impatience lay much fear and anxiety. Once she confronted these, allowing herself to sit quietly, feel them, and accept the fact that they were a part of her, she developed more patience and compassion for herself.

Set aside a day with no appointments. Wake up and sit quietly in bed for a while. Plan a day for yourself that has no errands or desk work on it. This is *your* day. Plan to do only things that make you feel wonderful. This is your reward. Clients who have tried this told me later that not having to be anywhere at a certain time was healing in itself.

Plan fewer things for the day. Don't make it a cardinal rule to call everyone back, especially people who waste your time. Don't feel you have to respond to people who get on your nerves—just listen and leave a lot of space.

Examine your expectations for yourself. Write down your personal expectations and talk them over with a supportive friend or confidante to gain an objective perspective. Are your expectations realistic? Most achievement addicts' problems lie not in what they do, but in how they measure themselves. If you bring your expectations into line with reality, you will regularly be pleased and rewarded instead of frustrated.

Don't worry. Letting go of your compulsion to achieve will not make you less able to accomplish what you set out to do. Achievement addicts never lose the ability to achieve. The difference is that you will begin to aim for satisfying goals, for accomplishments with real meaning for you—not for your parents or your boss or your spouse. The impulse to do more and more may always be there, but you will gain the ability to choose what is truly important to achieve and what isn't. You will begin to become more aware of where you want to spend your time, where you are out of balance, and when you need to relax and play. You will be able to achieve your objectives with less effort.

THE THIRD DEMON: THE BELIEF GAP

"You've got to know what you want to do in life, and then stick with it."

Just before he set himself up in his own consulting business, Jack told me, "I'm going to give this my best shot, but between you and me, I think 'consultant' is a euphemism for being unemployed. I'll be lucky if I don't starve."

A year later, this former vice president of advertising was making more money as a consultant than he ever dreamed possible and having more fun. His office was in his home and he looked more relaxed and younger than he had in years.

We all have ideas about the way the world works and assumptions about people, bosses, organizations, and ourselves that influence our thinking about our careers. When these beliefs are built on sound reasoning and experience, they can help us succeed. They can provide a solid basis for planning a crisis-proof career. Yet far too often, our beliefs are based on half-truths and outmoded ways of thinking that will sabotage our efforts.

After working with hundreds of people, I have seen many beliefs people cling to, convinced they are necessary for career success. Everyone has a personal "handbook" of policies and guidelines derived from personal experience, other people in their lives, and/or what they have seen and read. On the surface these beliefs seem plausible, and so we continue to hold on to them and act on them, unaware that they are false and in fact leave us vulnerable to self-endangerment.

What follows are some of the most common erroneous beliefs I hear. Check off the ones you feel are operating in your life. Try to reevaluate some of your own beliefs and, afterward, sit down with your notebook and compile a list. When you've written down ten or so beliefs, arrange to talk with a few friends about your personal "handbook" and see what they have to say. Offer to do the same for them. It can be fascinating to hear your friends' personal beliefs.

Exploding the Belief Gap

Belief #1: *Life success is equivalent to career success, which means upward mobility.*

Exploding Belief #1: Nothing could be further from the truth. Life success is the fulfillment of personally meaningful goals. You need to find out what brings *you* happiness. Your happiness may not come from upward mobility at all.

Take Amanda and Joe Harris, for example. They wanted to enjoy a quality lifestyle together, but they were burnt out working for a computer company, despite their high salaries. They sold their house, took all their savings, and moved to Mexico. Now they wake up each morning and ride their horses on the beach before settling down to work for the day at their own import-export business.

Reality #1: Life success is pursuing what you want in life and living by your own agenda.

Belief #2: *If you work hard and follow the rules, the company will take care of you.*

Exploding Belief #2: If you still believe this one, you haven't been paying attention. More than 6 million white-collar workers have been laid off since 1979. These are people who have logged in many years of experience with their employer.

Reality #2: Your only real security is your ability to adapt your skills to the needs of the marketplace and know how to market yourself.

Belief #3: *With an MBA you will always be able to get a job. It guarantees success.*

Exploding Belief #3: Currently there are many unemployed, experienced MBAs and others just out of the program who can't find work. Although a graduate degree puts you closer to the front of the line, it doesn't guarantee you a job.

Reality #3: Getting a graduate degree increases your value, but it doesn't insure job security.

Belief #4: *If I could only find out what I'm really good at, then I would know what career to pursue.*

Exploding Belief #4: Every day my clients tell me that they are good at many things, but that no one would pay them money to do them. On the other hand, they think the only employable skill they have is what they already get paid to do. What they fail to recognize is that if they spent time looking over all the skills they like to use (as in the Find Your Bliss Grid), they can put some of those together to form another career.

May loved to shop for clothes. She told me that when she was growing up, she and her family attended a church next door to Bloomingdale's. After worship, her mother and she would go shopping. To this day, May finds a deep satisfaction in shopping. She worked as a vice president for a large public relations firm, but toyed with the idea of starting her own business as an image consultant or a personal shopper. What stopped her was her realization that these services wouldn't earn her the same amount as her present job. Using some creative thinking, however, she and I were able to package her services in such a way as to match her present salary.

Reality #4: There are lots of things you can do to earn a good living if you are willing to reassess your career, do the necessary research, and take some risks.

Belief #5: *Somewhere out there is an exact answer to my dilemma of choosing a career that will perfectly fit with my interests, abilities, personality, and economic needs.*

Exploding Belief #5: Many people feel this way. They have the secret belief that somewhere along the way they made a tragic mistake and have wound up in the wrong career. Yet in all the hundreds of career tests I have administered, only about 15 percent revealed that the individual was actually in the wrong career. Others were simply in the wrong job setting. It may be the wrong fit of people, boss, career advancement, or job content that is driving you crazy.

It is also important to remember that we are living in turbulent and unstable times. No single answer is going to meet your needs from one year to the next. Rather, flexibility and an open mind will get you where you need to go.

Reality # 5: Your strongest asset is your ability to size up the situation and adapt to the changing environment.

Belief #6: *You should know exactly what you what to do in your career and do it!*

Exploding Belief #6: Virtually everyone I've met over thirty years old has said at one time or another, "I wonder what I want to be when I grow up?" Everything in our world is shifting and changing. What makes you think that you should be static? Even when we grow up, we keep on growing.

Reality #6: In this changing economy, the crisis-proof career seeker gets involved in growing. This involves staying in touch with what you need and want in your life so that you can take action to achieve it.

Belief #7: *The career decisions you make early in adulthood determine your success or failure in later life.*

Exploding Belief #7: Many of my clients have changed early career decisions into glorious triumphs in later years. Many have gone back to school for undergraduate degrees or taken their skills and transferred them into another industry or career. The later adult years are a time to shed outmoded careers and ways of being, to grow and find out more about yourself.

Reality #7: In this changing world you have two choices: grow or die.

Belief #8: *Fundamental career skills are acquired primarily in academic environments.*

Exploding Belief #8: Many clients tell me that they must go back to school to get another career, but this is not necessarily true. Many successful crisis-proofers have taken new jobs for the express purpose of learning a new skill, which they have then leveraged against their old skill to get the job they want.

Reality #8: There are many different ways to learn career skills, not just in school.

Belief #9: *Skills picked up in one field are only usable in that field; they are not transferable.*

Exploding Belief #9: Many skills are transferable. You need only demonstrate to a potential employer how those skills can benefit him or her.

For example, Bill has experience in data processing. He works in a bank. He can easily translate this skill into other service industries such as utilities, telephone, and cable television to get a broader range of jobs to choose from.

Gaye was in cellular-phone sales. She can apply her sales skills as a manufacturer's representative with product knowledge of appliances, clothes, and many consumer goods. All Bill and Gaye have to do is impress on a potential employer that they have what it takes.

Reality #9: Your major skill is your ability to sell your accomplishments to an employer and show him how you can get the job done.

Belief #10: *You should be able to find a job in the want ads.*

Exploding Belief #10: Want ads are the worst place to find jobs for two reasons. First, the number of candidates responding to any given want ad may be as high as 1,200. Why be one of the crowd?

Second, the jobs listed in the want ads are those that have inherent difficulties. If someone leaves a job, the employer's first tactic is to ask employees if they know of a qualified person to fill the vacancy. If the job has long hours, too much travel, or demanding customer contact, employees will come up empty-handed. The next line of defense for the employer is to contact a recruiter. However, recruiters charge between 25 and 33 percent of a potential candidate's total salary in fees. So a frugal employer will put an ad in a local or regional paper. Yet only 5 percent of all job searchers find jobs nationwide through want ads—even taking into account the high-level jobs listed in the *Wall Street Journal National Business Employment Weekly.*

Networking may require more effort then scanning the want ads, but your chances of finding something that you want are much, much higher. Not only are there fewer competitors, but you gain the added advantage of the credibility networking provides. By working through known contacts, people will have heard of you or know something about you and your history.

Reality #10: Networking is the best way to get a job because it gives you insight into a rapidly changing situation.

Belief #11: *Your friends don't really like to be asked for help or job leads.*

Exploding Belief #11: Most job hunters hate to ask friends for job leads because they hate to ask for help. Most of us were taught it is better to be self-sufficient. Yet friends are people who care about you and would like to be helpful. Give them the pleasure of assisting you.

Reality #11: Your best bet for leads are people who know you. There you have built-in credibility.

Belief #12: *I know what my skills are and what I'm good at.*

Exploding Belief #12: Most people have many more skills than they are aware of, although some skills may be rusty or untried. Our job often puts us into a very narrow focus as specialists, so that we never get to try other skills that we might have.

Reality #12: Crisis-proofers are willing to experiment and find out what hidden skills they might possess.

Belief #13: *It is important to keep your personal self and work self separate.*

Exploding Belief #13: Some of the best managers are ones who bring to work the interpersonal skills they learn away from work—with friends, for example, or in marriage and child rearing. A majority of people get fired not because they are incompetent, but because they lack the interpersonal skills to manage well. We do best when we bring all our talents to bear on whatever we do, personally or professionally.

Reality #13: It's how you work with people, not just what you know, that's important on the job.

Belief #14: *If I'm promoted on a regular basis, I know I'm succeeding.*

Exploding Belief #14: In this changing job climate, taking lateral promotions, accepting rotations that can mean learning new skills, and sometimes even taking a demotion can make you more marketable.

Reality #14: If you are at the middle of the organization or above, learning skills that make you more marketable is just as important in a changing economy as regular promotions.

Whether you are unemployed, thinking about a career or job change, or want to feel better in your current job, these reality checks of your beliefs are important. Without them, you may not be aware of current information on the changing job market. Don't be afraid to reassess your beliefs on an ongoing basis with friends, associates, and experts.

THE FOURTH DEMON: FEAR AS A SELF-IMPOSED BARRIER TO SUCCESS

"I'd like to start my own business, but I'm afraid I'd fail like my father."

Fear is a normal part of being alive. It's a natural emotion that warns us about danger and so has a purpose in our lives. We must remember, however, that fear can be irrational. We may fear something that is not dangerous, but simply uncomfortable or uncertain. There are many times in life when we must overcome our fear and take the next step.

If you feel you are not making progress in your job search, or if you have a dream but wonder why you are unable to implement it, it may be that fear is holding you back. Fear can be disguised in many forms that trick us into shunning risks and staying in our comfort zones. I have characterized some of the different forms as fear of embarrassment, fear of the unknown, lack of focus, and lack of commitment. Our purpose here is to show you how to recognize the particular barriers you are encountering as a result of your fear of risk. In later chapters I will show you how to devise a step-by-step career plan to overcome these barriers.

Fear of Embarrassment

Barry McKay was an energetic real estate developer in a medium-size leasing company. He looked like a leprechaun with his red hair and impish smile. When the department reorganized, he was asked to leave. Because of his effervescent personality and the type of work that he did, I assumed he would have no trouble talking to business acquaintances over the phone and conducting interviews. I soon learned otherwise.

In the context of his job, under the pressure of a demanding boss, Barry proved a tough negotiator who was able to make placements and close deals. When he had to call business acquaintances in this new context of looking for work, however, Barry couldn't do it. He came into the outplacement office, but he read newspapers all day. Sometimes he spent the precious time during working hours licking and stamping hundreds of envelopes with his resumé enclosed. I observed him waging this paper campaign and my heart sank. Experience has proven that it is virtually useless to send letters flying around or to occasionally pick up the phone and talk to someone's secretary. Barry and I had to have a heart-to-heart talk.

When we did, Barry confided how difficult it was for him to talk to people on the phone and ask for help. He couldn't understand why anyone would want to help him when he was just a "poor guy with his hat in hand." He was afraid that he would embarrass the other person, or he would come across as weak, needy, and helpless.

Barry saw business relationships as giving-and-receiving situations. If he was on the giving side, he felt in control, but when he was on the receiving side, he felt powerless. He needed to find a way to reframe business situations to see that in contacting people about his situation he was not using them for his own gain, but developing genuine relationships in which he could enjoy making contact with others. Out of that could flow genuine interest, rapport, trust, contacts, credibility, and perhaps even a job offer.

Most people who suffer from this fear of embarrassment fail to find satisfying work and never realize it. It stems from their difficulty with interpersonal relationships. You can be the smartest person in the world, but lack crucial social skills. This includes being sensitive to others, listening to the underlying messages of what is being said, giving and receiving criticism well, being emotionally stable, being sensitive to nonverbal cues and body language, and building support for yourself and others.

The origin of this fear usually lies in one's past where there was an experience or many experiences in which you were humiliated in front of people. Perhaps a teacher humiliated you in front of the class, or a parent shamed you in front of your friends. Whether or not you can remember the situation, these childhood experiences make it difficult not to fear embarrassment and humiliation.

Barry and I constructed a telephone script to get him started. We developed answers to the most difficult questions he thought he would face in an interview. We developed a career plan (like the ones in later chapters of this book) covering the next several years, which he could discuss clearly and confidently in a face-to-face meeting. We thought of all the reasons why others would want to talk to him, despite the fact that he was currently unemployed.

Barry soon found he was able to build rapport and trust along with the best of them, and he was no longer limited by this self-imposed barrier.

Fear of the Unknown

Connie Light always wanted to start her own business. She worked for many years at a large and prestigious marketing-research consulting firm. She had the longest tenure of any of the fifteen associates. Yet she felt that her ideas were often watered down and her creativity was squelched. She knew she had gone about as far as she could in that company. The next step was being a star herself and standing behind her own ideas.

Finally Connie had saved enough money to take a year off and start building her business, and she knew her dream had the possibility of becoming a reality. Then she hesitated. All of a sudden she was immobilized, afraid to take a chance. She heard her mother's voice saying, "It's better to be secure than take a risk." How many times had she heard that little voice inside her head? Then she heard her father's voice, "You get a good job and work hard, and you are set for life." She began to feel that she could never be free to be herself and have what she wanted.

"I am afraid to take the plunge. What happens if I fail? I may not have what it takes." She could glibly discuss her glamorous vision of her future to her friends, but it was after those times that she hated herself most because she knew she didn't have the nerve to start her new business.

Then the managing partner suffered a heart attack and died. Her male colleague, ten years her junior with less tenure in the firm, was named for the vacancy. Connie was furious. Her anger finally gave her the impetus to leave. Just then, however, she received an offer from a competitor based on the East Coast. They wanted her to open and manage the West Coast office of their firm. The salary and perquisites would be commensurate with the position. Once again Connie hesitated. This new offer immobilized her again.

As we worked together sorting through her dilemma, Connie realized that there would always be many options available to her. In turning down this one option, she was not deciding against all future offers.

When we have a decision to make, we, like Connie, may see only a single fork in the road. We believe that we must choose either the right or the left, and our lives will be forever changed as a result. Yet we really have many options all the time, although we may be too scared to see them. Sometimes the options are small, but if we can take a single step, we may find it frees us to do much more. When we try something new, take a small risk, even more options become available. The unknown becomes less scary.

There will always be comfort in complaining and blaming and staying risk-averse. But if you choose to stay in your comfort zone, to remain immobilized, you give up control of your life to others. I helped Connie see possibilities in each situation, lower her fear by generating a list of options and obstacles (as we will do in chapter 5), and once again take charge of her life. She chose to open her own business and assume the responsibility for realizing her own dream.

Lack of Focus

Fear of risk can take many different forms. For Connie, it was immobilization: she could choose what she wanted but not act on it. Another form is lack of focus. This issue usually surfaces in people who have a lot of energy, creativity, and brilliance.

Ken Carty chooses again and again. Each time the choice is wholehearted—it just doesn't last long because he doesn't choose carefully enough.

Ken was a top real estate agent in the biggest office in town. When the market went soft, he decided that it was a good time to try something new. He began working as a recruiter, but after three months he told me, "This is just as hard as real estate; maybe I should go back to that, after all. It's so hard to place people. I'm used to getting big bucks and it takes forever to place just one person. Also, houses don't talk, people do. They also change their minds; they decide not to leave their jobs or they don't show up for interviews. People are too complex for me!"

So Ken decided to go into the computer business because he saw people making lots of money at it. He was hired by a computer retailer as a salesperson. Three months later he called me to complain. "I didn't realize how hard this is. Sure I've made some little sales, but this is nickel-and-dime compared to selling a house or property. Or recruiting, at least I can talk about people. Here if people get technical on me, I'm dead and then I lose the sale."

Like so many people with this problem Ken became frustrated when good fortune didn't shine immediately on each new endeavor. He was unwilling to start at the beginning, roll up his sleeves, and gradually learn the ropes. To find what we are best suited for and what we really want to do, we have to stifle our impulses and replace action with careful planning. Ken and I went to work on the planning of his crisis-proof career plan, and we were able to find the right fit for Ken. With a long-term career plan, he knew where he was headed and could know what to expect in terms of progress.

Lack of Commitment

Commitment is investing our energy and time in what we do and participating 100 percent. When we lack commitment, it is generally because we feel that we can protect ourselves from failure by not getting involved emotionally. Frank Townsend suffered from fear of commitment.

I met Frank two years ago, when he was managing partner of a large investment-banking firm. He was among the best and brightest out of Stanford and came from a wealthy California family. Problems arose when Frank began getting signals from his boss that the investment firm was not happy with him. In fact, they hadn't been happy with his performance for some time, but business had been good and he had been there so long that no one wanted to confront the issue of Frank Townsend.

Now with the slumping economy, Frank was asked to leave. Frank and I spent many hours reviewing his career and his life. He slowly revealed to me that he had never been very invested in the firm emotionally. The way he avoided failure was by not involving himself in the decisions of the firm, taking the lesser clients, and staying in the background. Over the years, these actions defined him to others.

"I don't feel as if I am using my potential; I feel as if I have failed in my own expectations of myself. When I used to think of myself at this age, I thought I would be doing something that had an impact on humanity. But I'm just matching companies and money. Big deal!" For many months we worked long and hard. Frank found several companies that matched his criteria for fulfillment. He put together a short-term and a long-term plan, but the first step never materialized. As Frank got closer to an offer, his list of criteria became longer and more nonnegotiable. No one could ever match what Frank wanted. It was only after he faced his lack of commitment that he was truly able to commit to a course of action and implement his career plans.

A fear of commitment is perhaps the most deadly of all, because it is not simply your failure to commit to a plan of action—more importantly it is a failure to commit to yourself, your hopes, and your dreams. Underlying a lack of commitment is low self-esteem. To be successful you have to believe that you deserve success. You have to have an image of yourself so tangible that you can reach out and touch it.

CHALLENGING THE DEMONS

Knowing you deserve something better is a way of challenging your fears. You need to challenge the small voice inside your head that says, "I can't," or "I don't deserve this." Self-defeating thoughts, belief gaps, and self-imposed barriers to success are judgments about your reality. You have the power to reorient your thinking so you can envision a creative, satisfying future.

To do this, you must accept change. Frequently this requires living in a state of uncertainty. For many in the midst of a job transition, it involves accepting your own vulnerability. Change involves risking and stretching. It is not the change or the transition but how you cope with it that determines the kind of person you become. As Nietzsche said, "That which does not kill us makes us stronger."

All these inner demons have one thing in common: fear. Fear generates self-defeating thoughts, fear causes us to cling to false beliefs, fear creates the achievement addict. These self-imposed barriers keep us safe because they stop us from taking the risks we fear but need to take to grow. Eventually, they keep us from our dreams and the fulfillment of our potential.

At the same time, these barriers can't save us from the loss of our job or dissatisfaction with our lives, but they can prohibit us from reaching out beyond the loss and dissatisfaction, if we let them. Growth, belief in oneself, and a willingness to attempt the unattempted are key ingredients to achieving the crisis-proof career.

WHAT'S REALLY IMPORTANT?

Almost every day for three years, Alan and I would pass each other on the jogging path, and he would always say hello. Other times, I'd see him on the ferry going to his job as president of a retail chain. Then one day he ran right past me on the trail and didn't even look my way. Later at the local bakery, a mutual friend told me Alan had lost his job. When I tried to call Alan, I learned his phone number had been taken out of service.

When people lose their jobs, they are stripped of their image of who they are. It's a painful event that often fills them with terror, but it is also quite compelling because they temporarily acquire a certain vulnerability. They are forced to give up some of the illusions they had about themselves and their position in the world. Outside the comfort zone they can acquire a new perspective on themselves and their careers. They may feel as if they are dying, but in many ways it is a golden opportunity.

In my experience, the most rewarding approach to this painful time is to embrace the terror and turn that frightening energy into creative effort. Don't let yourself be paralyzed by the fear: the fear of the unknown, fear to tell people what happened, fear to talk to strangers on the phone, fear of interviewing, fear of discovering what you do best, fear of failing, and fear of being fully alive. That is what conquering the demons within is all about: conquering the fear.

Sometimes I think we've been brainwashed into believing that life is the way it is portrayed in movies or on television. On the weekly television series the heroine marries, divorces, becomes queen of a foreign country, and goes to jail all in one hour. We've come to believe that our successes happen overnight, and only because of blind luck. Our self-esteem is measured by symbols: we are our cars, our credit cards, our job titles. Take away all the tangible evidence of success and we feel worthless.

During these transitions, I remind my clients of their best qualities and of other races they have run and won. I believe in them when they may momentarily be incapable of believing in themselves. The source of their past and future success is not the success itself, but the person who created it, and who can create it again step by step.

One client confessed that he thought the process of working with me was just an exercise, meaningless and ordinary, and he just wanted to get through it and get another job. Unfortunately, I have seen many like him, and they seem to stay unemployed for an extraordinarily long time. This "exercise" is meant to engage the individual on a deeper level, and if it is not used to learn some of life's most difficult lessons, or to find the inner resources to discover what we want for ourselves, the job search continues without success.

The tide turns when the client begins to enjoy the journey, when he or she realizes it's really not about finding the right job but about finding oneself and expressing that self in a truly creative way. Out of this experience, the question emerges: "What is really important to do?" I don't think the world is ever the same for my clients after they face this crisis of values and confidence.

At the same time as I encourage clients to open to the pain, I also encourage them to create a vision. People can easily tell you what they don't want, or what they might settle for, because the mind has a great ability to catastrophize. "I can always get a job pumping gas," one former vice president of an insurance company said to me. "I can go back to being a computer programmer," said an executive vice president of management information services. It takes long hours and some difficult questions before clients can begin to replace these negative images and gain a glimpse of what has meaning and purpose for them in the second half of their lives. I ask them, what has life for them, what is significant, and what makes them feel alive and challenged? That, I tell them, is what is really important.

TELLING YOURSELF THE TRUTH

The most important thing in crisis-proofing your career is to be honest with yourself. You need to confront the demons where you find them and tackle the thoughts and patterns that keep you from getting where you need to go. Without awareness of the demons within, you cannot help but transfer a certain desperation to the job search.

Your successful career begins with you, and no one else. Conversely, it may be said that you are its only saboteur. You have to believe you can do it. You must have an internal vision of success that drives you in a focused, enduring way. Toy inventor Carl Walters described this feeling perfectly: "I work alone. I have no support group of coworkers or a company to go to. I only have my desk and phone in the basement of the house. Each morning I wake up with a vision of who I am and my contribution in the world. I feel like I go forth like a crusader with a banner unfurled. I go out into the world. I am a toy maker, I am an inventor. I stimulate and mold small, vulnerable minds."

People who have conquered the demons within can speak up and take a stand. "What other people think of me is nobody's business," as evangelist Terry Cole Whitaker said. Crisis-proofers project their own convictions of their worth and so convince others. This is the indefinable quality that employers look for in an interview with candidates. This is the "sizzle" bosses look for when considering employees for promotion.

The demons can be conquered by generating options and opening the box each of us lives in. By using the tools described in this chapter you can begin to overcome the demons. In the next chapter I'll describe some creative ways of generating options and putting into action a crisis-proof career strategy.

## CHAPTER 5

EXPANDING THE HORIZONS
EXERCISES IN OPTIONS

*H*ow many times have you sat in a darkened theater watching a play or movie and became so involved in the story that you lost track of everything but the adventure unfolding before you? One magical quality of movies, plays, and books is their ability to show us new worlds and possibilities unimaginable in our own lives. Through characters we can vicariously experience new ways of being, try on different roles, and see life through different eyes.

As children, before we assumed our real-life adult roles, we often played this game of pretend. Imagining new possibilities for ourselves was something we did every day. We would be seafarers one day and play house the next, cast ourselves as imperious kings and queens one time and poor orphans another. We traveled to any exotic land we could think of, doing and being anything we wanted.

As we mature, we are taught to put away this imaginative, childlike self and allow the adult to take over. The curious, playful, and wonderfully expansive part of us is replaced by the grown-up who hates risks and despises uncertainty. The adult seeks out comfort zones to protect against setbacks and disappointments. The childlike part is still inside, of course, but most of us ignore its wishes and demands. We may feel this conflict between the child and the adult when part of us wants to explore something new and another part wants to play it safe.

The search for a crisis-proof career requires both curiosity and practicality. To find what is truly meaningful in our lives requires us to engage both aspects of ourselves, the child and the adult. Before we can find where we belong, we need to explore many options, imagine a variety of roles, and combine the best aspects of each. In this process, we have a great deal to learn from the childlike part of ourselves; indeed, its input is essential if we are to succeed in building a crisis-proof career.

In this chapter, I will reacquaint you with this childlike part through a variety of exercises designed to free you from your comfort zone. If you allow them, these exercises can help you find what is missing from your present situation so that you can begin to incorporate these missing pieces.

ABOUT CREATIVE THINKING

Most people don't feel particularly creative. We associate creativity with the performing arts, or the work done alone by starving artists. Some people may feel that the family allotment of creativity passed them by and went to their brother or cousin instead.

On the contrary, being creative is about bringing your best to each moment. It is a way of thinking about yourself and your interactions with the world. All of us have the ability to create something out of nothingness. We can all take an old idea and find a new twist on it, use limited resources in a new way, find how to do more with less, or discover a need where no one saw one before. This is creativity, and this is what most people do at their jobs and in their personal lives every day. People who fool themselves by thinking that they are not particularly creative nonetheless express themselves in their dress, hobbies, lifestyle, and thinking.

Read this chapter with the knowledge that you are creative and that the childlike part of yourself needs only some encouragement to reappear. The child lets someone else worry about the money, time, and security while he or she is off on an adventure being this or that. Give your adult side a day or two off and allow the child to run free.

After many years of helping clients build more productive and satisfying careers, I've learned that creative thinking involves uncontrollable forces. No matter what we do, there will be barren as well as fertile times. Yet we can make the barren times more productive by using them to prepare for the insights to come.

Here are some guidelines to keep in mind as you prepare to think creatively about your career.

1. Creativity and criticism cannot operate successfully at the same time. To be creative, you need to stop comparing yourself to others and stop criticizing your efforts.

2. Persistence pays. If you work steadily at the exercises in this chapter, you will see results. Genius is 90 percent sweat and 10 percent inspiration.

3. Get rid of the great misconception that you must have an idea before you can create, or know what you're doing before you start. Creative thinking springs from your curiosity, passion, and trusting the process. As children, my brother and I played with his Erector set. Sometimes we would set out to build one thing, and before we knew it, it had grown into something far better. If we had stuck to our original ideas, some of our best creations would never have been built.

The creative process is not as mysterious as you may have been led to believe. In fact, researchers have found creativity occurs in four stages. The first stage is *preparation*. Here we define the problem, break it into its component parts, and focus our attention on the available options. We may define, organize, gather information, dream, and write about the problem for which we need a solution.

Then, when we are saturated with this information, the next phase begins. Researchers call this the *incubation* stage. This involves putting the problem aside for a time, taking our mind off it by going for a walk, reading the newspaper, or dining with friends. You may be aware of it hovering at the back of your mind, but you can allow it to remain there while you are involved with other activities.

Sooner or later—usually later—stage three of the process occurs. Without conscious manipulation, you perceive some insights, associations, and images that come to mind when you least expect them. Suddenly what had seemed unsolvable has a solution. What was obscure is now transparent. Researchers fittingly call this the *illumination* stage. It can happen in a dream, while you are taking a shower, or even brushing your teeth. It can happen when you are sitting at your desk doing something completely different. Write down the thought at your earliest opportunity. Don't judge it yet, just record it for later. The idea may seem so simple, you don't trust it. Record everything you can, staying with it for a few minutes to expand on any particular parts.

Then you come to the final stage, *verification*. Here you examine your insights and see whether they are reasonable and feasible. Do they provide the solution (or a partial solution) to the problem? Sometimes they don't, and then it's back to the drawing board. At other times, these become the basis for later insights. All is grist for the mill.

In this four-stage process, effort counts, but so does letting go. If you're unaccustomed to letting go, this may be the hardest part. Yet without some space for entertaining the ridiculous, encouraging your playfulness, being spontaneous, true creativity cannot happen. Throughout this process you must learn to trust the void.

When I ask people about their career, they become linear and analytical. The adult part is in control. They rationally compartmentalize working and money in one corner, and play and fun in the other. My dad would agree. He used to say, "Work is supposed to be just that, work! It's a rare person who can make their vocation their avocation." Yet this is just what crisis-proofers do.

LIVING FOR SURVIVAL — OR CREATIVITY?

If you are like most people, your career has been spent learning how to survive, being concerned about your safety and security. What if, just for the moment, you *stopped* worrying about survival and started thinking about another way of looking at your career? Think about what inspires you and makes you feel good. Just imagine that the money will come either way. Hold that thought as you work through the exercises in this chapter. Don't be too critical—later on in the chapter, I'll show you how to handle the critic in you.

Even if you don't think of yourself as particularly creative, you probably know the conditions in which you do your best thinking. Most of us do, but we are often too stingy to permit ourselves to enjoy them. We think we are being self-indulgent if we seek out these conditions. As you work with the exercises in this chapter, consciously create those conditions for yourself as often as possible, building in time every day where you are in your most creative setting. Take a relaxed walk, turn on some music and move around the living room, daydream over coffee before breakfast.

The best in ourselves is motivated not by what we perceive ourselves to be, but by what we believe we can be. In a competitive and bottom-line society, we need more than ever to allow ourselves to daydream, reach out, and explore new options. The rosy visions we had as young people about ourselves, our future careers, the ways in which we hoped one day to live, are as important to a successful life as concrete skill development. Building a picture of what we *really* want in our lives is an important part in crisis-proofing a career. We can choose to be motivated either by fearful thoughts or by creative thoughts.

When Heather was completing her doctorate in psychology, she would frequently pass Belchertown State School. Every time she did, she would think about others she knew who had gotten their PhD only to end up with jobs at Belchertown. There they earned minimum wage changing the diapers of mentally retarded adults. "I probably will, too," she thought.

This picture of her future depressed Heather until one day she realized that she could choose to picture any kind of future she wanted. She began to think of how she could finally move to Boston, rent her own apartment, and live alone for the first time—no more roommates. She thought about getting a job teaching graduate school in Cambridge. Every time she caught herself looking at Belchertown State School, she would picture this alternative future. She was so excited with her new ideas she began to tell her friends and family about them, too.

Several months later, her roommate saw an advertisement for a position as a professor in a graduate school in Cambridge. Her roommate came running into Heather's office waving the ad and shouting, "You're a natural for this job!" Sure enough, Heather applied for and got the job.

If Heather had filled her thoughts with Belchertown, she would not have made the effort to find something better. She would never have told her friends and set in motion the events that eventually led to the fulfillment of her dreams.

Here are some exercises designed to expand your linear ways of thinking about yourself, just as Heather did. These imaginative exercises teach valuable lessons about new options and expanded horizons. They are lessons in hope, vision, and wishes come true.

CAREER AEROBICS: WARM-UP AND STRETCHING PHASE

Aerobics bring oxygen to the body, strengthening lungs and heart, and fortifying the spirit. If done for twenty minutes or more, aerobics will burn away fatty tissue. I call the following exercises "career aerobics" because they exercise the imagination. If you do these exercises on a daily basis, they will prevent hardening of the creative arteries and open your mind to options, possibilities, and opportunities in your journey to find meaningful work.

For many of these exercises, you can use your loose-leaf notebook and a pen or pencil to record your answers. For others, crayons or colored pencils enhance the fun.

Getting It All Out!

This is a physical-stress reliever to get you started. Stand up wherever you are and shake your arms and legs. Use words and sounds to wipe, pull, or push away all the negative things that made up your day. Imagine all the pet peeves, irritations, and difficult people you dealt with. Imagine that they form a physical substance that you can take and shape into a toxic ball. Go ahead and form this imaginary ball, and as it grows bigger, push or throw it out the door or window. Yell or shout it out, if you want.

Now take a deep breath. See how good it feels to be free of them all. Free from the stress of the day, you are ready to work.

The Question-and-Answer Game

In the spirit of play, let's make believe you know all the answers to your future; you simply lack the ability to know these answers on a conscious level.

On a piece of paper, write down an open-ended career question starting with *who, what, why* or *how,* but not a question that requires a yes or no answer. Immediately write down the first answer that comes to mind. Then write another question that comes out of the first response, answer it, then try another question. Keep going. See if you can fill two whole pages with questions and their answers.

For example, "What is missing in my work right now?"

Answer: "Some time off."

"Why do you say that?"

"Because you look and feel tired lately."

Other good questions might be: What will my next boss be like? What do I see myself doing next year at this time? Why can't I find what I want? What is holding me back? How can I ask for help from friends?

For a variation, play this game with a friend or your children. They can help you get in the spirit of the game.

One night not long ago, a client of mine tried this. The next morning she came in glowing:

"I've finally understood my fears about leaving my company. This technique helped because I let a part of myself answer without censoring it. I guess I really did know the answers."

Someone I Admire

Choose a person you admire, who you feel would deserve to be featured on the cover of *Time* magazine as man or woman of the year. Describe this person and why you admire him or her. Is it his or her personal life or public career, talents, skills, or personality? Write it as if you were that person. For example:

> *My name is Barbara Walters. I am strong and accomplished. I'm close to seventy, but I appear young and vital. I know who I am. Even Fidel Castro became my admirer when I went to interview him in Cuba.*

Or, what about this one?

> *My name is Cher. I am popular, and I am well connected. I never have to worry about making a living, and everyone wants to help me.*

Someone I Envy

Choose a friend or acquaintance whom you envy or feel jealous of in some way. Write down why you envy this person, writing again in the first person, as if you were him or her.

I am my friend Sonja, who makes writing books seem so effortless. I am very slim. I am attractive and never have to worry about food, because eating is not the "face entertainment" it is to the real me.

Rewriting My Childhood Story

Often when people ask us where we were born and raised, we wish we didn't have to tell the truth. After all, who wants to be born in Newark, New Jersey, when there are so many other, more interesting places to come from? At least that is how I felt. My childhood was so ordinary. So I decided some years ago to make up a story that made me feel good when I told it to my friends (who were kind enough to play along). I invite you to try it, too. Make up a new, better life story, leaving out the parts you didn't like and adding the parts you would. The purpose of the exercise is to help you see that you are not tied to the same old reality, but can begin to recast your self-image and open up to new possibilities.

Here's Sally's:

I was born at the Dakota Apartments in Manhattan, two doors down from where John Lennon and Yoko Ono lived. In fact, the Lennons were our neighbors. (More about that later, if you ask.) My mom was a movie star and my dad was the president of a large conglomerate. I had fun with my brothers and sisters. We got along famously and we were a very artistic family. In fact, every summer we all hopped on an airplane to Paris where we attended the de'Coeur Art School.

The story goes on, but you get the idea. Sally was really born and raised in Detroit, the only daughter of an assembly-line worker.

Postcards From the Other Side

Sometimes what we value at one point in our lives appears very different years later. In the end, what will you want to be remembered for? What, in the last analysis, will have the most meaning for you? Make up a short postcard to send to a loved one to read at your memorial service or a year or two after you are gone.

Brian wrote this imaginary message to his wife: "I loved you very deeply, and I wanted never to disappoint you. I tried to be loving in all that I did and said. I also wanted to make a contribution to the world with my music."

Mary wrote an imaginary postcard to her mom: "I surprised you, didn't I? You wanted me to marry a doctor, but I became one instead. I spent my life surprising everyone, but mostly myself, with my talents. I really enjoyed my life and want you to know the adventure continues on the other side."

Your Favorite Fairy Tale

Choose a fairy tale or any other story that you liked as a child. Write down a brief plot synopsis and then explain what about it appealed to you, and why you liked it so much. What happened in it that you would like to happen to you? What was the happy ending, if there was one, and how does that resemble your own dream of a "happy ending"?

Sally chose "Cinderella." She loved how the prince came and discovered Cinderella and saved her from the wicked stepsisters. Sally often wished she could just pick up and leave all the responsibilities that kept her living in the same old apartment, working at the same job in the same city. She was looking for someone who would take her away from it all. Describing the story, Sally started to think about her own "rescue." She began to consider more seriously what she could do for herself instead of waiting for her "prince."

Brian's favorite fairy tale was "Jack and the Beanstalk." He loved the way Jack screwed up his courage and climbed that beanstalk. Brian realized that courage was a trait he had always admired in others and that he needed courage in his life.

How to Make Sense Out of the Warm-up

Look over all the warm-up exercises you've made in your notebook as if you were a private detective searching for clues. Look for common themes or patterns. Then take your notebook and pencil and answer the following questions as best you can. (If you have trouble, show your answers to a friend and invite him or her to help you.)

1.   What words do I find myself using most often? What does my

choice of language say about the parts of me that are not expressed in my life? (Look for words that indicate missing elements, such as *time off, play, freedom, family,* or *leisure.*)

2.   What values are being revealed in what I say about myself? (You may want to go back into chapter 3 and look at The Values Indicator.)

3.   What experiences am I yearning for? What am I seeking?

4.   What concerns, fears, or apprehensions come to the surface when I do these exercises?

THE CAREER AEROBIC PHASE

Now that you've used the warm-up phase to limber up your right-brain thinking, it is time to begin the Career Aerobic Phase in earnest. For this we must return to more substantive aspects of your life and learn what the past can reveal about the present.

Career Lifeline

Get a sheet of paper and art supplies, such as colorful Magic Markers, crayons, or colored pencils. You may want to use two clean pages of notebook paper or a child's oversize newsprint tablet. Now draw a picture representing your life up to the present. Use whatever symbol you feel appropriate: a tree with branches, a graph with ups and downs, a straight line, a bell-shaped curve, a steep mountain with peaks and valleys. Then mark off five-year intervals. Think back to each of these five-year intervals and ask what values dominated that time of your life. Now take your crayons and draw the following for each of these five-year periods:

1.   The experiences that affected you or molded you.

2.   The people who influenced you, positively or negatively.

3.   Periods you felt connected through a sense of community and relationships.

4.   Periods of great achievement and creativity.

5.   Put stars next to the times when you felt especially valued, appreciated, significant.

Some people let their imaginations go and draw all kinds of

images and impressions. Others do a more linear chart with time as one dimension and the events, people, values, achievement, and affiliation during each five-year interval as offshoots of the central lifeline. Find a way that suits your style.

When Ray did the exercise, it looked like a stock market report: every five years there were peaks and valleys. Pearl drew hers like a mandala, while Bonnie portrayed a spiral. There is no right answer.

Remember, this is simply a process of inquiry. Everyone has a different set of experiences and different things to say and draw. This process may set you off into a trajectory of new inquiry about some common themes and patterns in your life.

For example, Ray saw how he used achievement as a way of warding off loneliness. Pearl saw how she used men as anchors in her life during periods of stress.

Jot down the themes and patterns you see. How do they compare or contrast with what you learned in the career aerobic warm-up phase?

When I'm at My Best

Select five themes that run throughout your lifeline, such as work, family, religion, relationships, physical self, financial situation, creative self, health, and friendships. You can use any of the areas listed in The Satisfaction Indicator or The Values Indicator (in chapter 3). Then write a story about the time in your life when you were at your best in each of these areas. What were you doing, who was there, how did it begin, how did it end, when were you feeling most creative? Determine if it was the setting that inspired you to work at your best or the skills you employed during those times. Write about a page on each.

For example: Pearl wrote on "Personal Development." Thinking back, she felt she made the most progress in this area during the five-year period around her divorce. It was a period when she remembers actively making improvements in her life, taking care of her own needs, and doing things the way she wanted them done. From this story, Pearl gained a very clear sense that she was at her best when she asserted her autonomy and stood up for herself, instead of using the men in her life as a crutch, as she had a tendency to do. She realized that she enjoyed her freedom and she resolved never to give it away again.

"Today I Am..." Visualization

What would you do if you were suddenly independently wealthy? How would you spend your life if you had nothing to do but fulfill the dreams you've harbored for so long? For some, one particular thought or fantasy takes precedence; others have many different ideas of what they would like to do. Without an outlet in which to explore these thoughts, we have no way to sort them out. When we do, we can find out what will inspire us and learn more about our essential self.

When I first met Dan, his office looked as if he were planning a vacation. There were posters all over the walls and ceilings. "No," he replied to my question, "these are just all my escape fantasies. I never get enough time off to ever do these things." So Dan and I invented a game to explore all the possibilities he could think of to do and see.

Just complete the sentence "Today I am..." and describe a role to play that day, that week, or that year. For example, "Today I am...a world traveler. I am traveling to all the spiritual shrines in the world. I'll do this for a year, until I get tired, and then I'll come home."

Here are some rules to follow to keep you on track:

1. It must be something that gives you a pleasant feeling while you are thinking about it.
2. It doesn't actually have to be something you are going to do or even would really want to do. You are simply expressing yourself.
3. Describe everything in the present tense as if it were already happening.
4. Put all the niggling details aside (like what to do with your husband or kids or who will pay the mortgage).
5. Let yourself go and just daydream. Do not shoot down your dream with criticism.
6. Create as many different roles for yourself as you like. You may want to do this over a period of several weeks.

I suggest you try doing these "Today I Am..." visualizations in the shower each morning or in your car or on the bus on the way to work. Finding a particular place you go every day where you are alone is best because it helps you get into the right frame of mind. The more you do it, the easier it will become. Then, plan a time each day where you can write out your visualization for closer consideration.

For inspiration, turn to your answers to the Find Your Bliss Grid in chapter 3. Let your imagination seize on a different item each day to elaborate and explore.

Here are examples of what three of my clients came up with. Each has its own personality and themes. Can you recognize what qualities are given expression in each of these dreams?

Carl—The first day in the shower:

Today I am... president of my own real estate consulting firm. We have offices in eight major metropolitan areas and are considered to be the finest location specialists in the United States. I am meeting with our city presidents to review a major marketing opportunity. Other items on my calendar are to meet with the head of the California Economic Development Commission to talk about emerging trends. In the afternoon I will be working with our director of research on a new analytical tool for siting firms, speaking at a weekly training session for consultants on interpersonal selling skills, and visiting with major clients on one of our regular client satisfaction audits. This evening my wife and I will be guests of the Gettys at the opening of a small avant-garde theater in the Mission district of San Francisco.

Carl—The second day in the shower:

Today I am... a successful developer of a number of innovative mixed-use buildings that have won awards and earned high returns on our investors' dollars. I am meeting with the management team for our next undertaking—a $250-million redevelopment of the Navy Pier area in San Francisco. For lunch I am meeting with the mayor and several members of the Board of Supervisors to talk about job creation in the city based on a report from a task force I chaired at the mayor's request. The afternoon will be spent playing tennis with three of my best friends. In the evening I will be meeting with three other trustees for Stanford University to discuss our recommendations on the law school's mission to the year 2010.

Carl—The third day in the shower:

Today I am... independently wealthy and am chairman of Common Cause, which I have revitalized as a citizen's lobbying group for "good government." I am meeting with one of the advisory panels on the reform of the state mental health programs. Our recommendations have been adopted by five state legislatures and we are evaluating the success of our strategy in the bellwether states. For lunch I will be talking with the secretary of health and welfare on a variety of topics of mutual interest. In the afternoon there are a series of legislative review sessions with staff heads. This evening my wife and I will be attending a Latin music performance to benefit the Northeast Washington Economic Development Council, which a friend has organized.

Carl—The fourth day in the shower:

Today I am . . . independently wealthy and governor of California. I am making a speech to the leadership of the state Senate and Assembly on the need for a number of education programs that will improve the management and quality of the teaching in the public school system. Later in the morning I am working with the director of planning and research on the long-range economic development plan for California. Lunch is with a group of prominent business leaders with whom I have been meeting to discuss issues of mutual concern. The afternoon is filled with a number of policy sessions with key aides and department staff. At five o'clock Leslie and I will board a plane for Hawaii for the National Governor's Meeting and a vacation at our secluded beach house on Kauai.

Carl's values and needs are reflected in his four daydreams in the shower. Four common threads are his need for recognition, achievement, power, and money. Carl and I then discussed the fact that these needs were not being met in his life. That gave us some good clues as to where Carl should start making some changes in his life.

Robin's daydreams were somewhat different from Carl's:

Robin—First day on the bus:

Today I am . . . a brilliant theologian and biblical scholar for the Union Theological Seminary. Everyone is asking for more information about my unique interpretation of the Dead Sea Scrolls.

Robin—Second day on the bus:

Today I am . . . a writer for the Boston Globe, *packing to go to my house in Nantucket to write a winsome summer reverie on the great whaling ships of the nineteenth century.*

Robin—Third day on the bus:

Today I am ... head of curriculum development for the State of California, lecturing on how to incorporate the Socratic method into teaching models in the public school system.

Robin—Fourth day on the bus:

Today I am ... the producer of the Olympic games, conferring with major corporations regarding their sponsorships, making deals on ad time for underwriting support, and designing the logo for the XYZ corporation Olympic-jacket sportswear line.

Robin—Fifth day on the bus:

Today I am ... the director of the Metropolitan Opera. My office in Lincoln Center is full of antiques, and I travel frequently to Italy to recruit singers.

Robin—Sixth day on the bus:

Today I am ... a decorator of historic residences, researching antique French chairs for a château in southern France.

When Robin examined the nature of her daydreams, she recognized a desire to help people in artistic, humanitarian, and rather idealistic ways. She would enjoy taking the lead and using her creativity to win recognition and acclaim for her personal excellence.

Sometimes clients are afraid that they will go on indefinitely with new and expansive daydreams, never reaching an end and never addressing all the needs that they have. Yet they find that after doing these exercises for a time that the daydreams begin to build on one another and become more and more consistently one exciting dream. The elements just naturally flow together into one compelling career idea.

After you have practiced the "Today I Am..." visualization for several weeks, reread what you have written. Refer back to the Values Indicator in chapter 3 for an idea of the types of themes you may detect in your entries. How do you interpret what you wrote? Look for the feelings and emotions you experience when you think about these daydreams. What are some common threads, common values? How would you feel about taking action on one of them and actually doing that as a career? Could you combine two or more? When you think about acting on any of these fantasies, consider what you would need to change about your life. What trade-offs would you have to make? What would you be willing to give up?

The Quality of Experience

When we know what we want in our lives, we often set a goal and measure ourselves by our progress toward it. As time goes on, we may forget what it was about the goal that led us to choose it in the first place. It is important not only to identify the goals, but the quality of the experience we expect to derive from reaching them. In many cases, the quality of experience can be found to derive from reaching them. In many cases, the quality of experience can be found in other ways, perhaps as a part of our life in a form we have not yet realized. When we consider this possibility, it becomes another way of opening ourselves to greater flexibility and increases our chances of getting what we want.

A divorced mother of two, Debra was celebrating her fortieth birthday the week she confided to me that in all her "Today I am..." daydreams she was married. "That is what I miss in my life," she said, "being married." I asked her to imagine I was a Martian from outer space and had no idea of what marriage meant.

"Well," she said, "being married means being emotionally close or intimate with someone, sharing common interests and having common goals." Then I asked her if she didn't already have some of these qualities in her life. Perhaps by expecting only marriage to provide them, she was rejecting the closeness and intimacy she already shared with the people in her life. When she thought about it, Debra agreed. She already enjoyed this emotional closeness with her children and her friends. More importantly, she saw that she could cultivate it more deeply in those places, rather than waiting for a single relationship to supply it.

Now reread your daydreams and list the *qualities* of the experience you are seeking. Where are these qualities already present in your life? Where could you go and what could you do to increase the likelihood of finding these qualities? What would be the trade-offs? Are you willing to make them? If not, why not?

The Free-to-Succeed Society

What would you choose to do if time and money were no object and your success were guaranteed? If you didn't have to pay the mortgage, worry about sending the kids to college, or make payments on your car, what could you do to bring you joy?

Imagine there is a private foundation looking for life dreams to fund. All you need to do to receive an annual grant of $2 million is to write out a detailed description of your dream and submit it. All applications are preapproved. You cannot be turned down.

After the typical images of traveling, vacations, and endless games of golf or tennis, we begin to ask what's *really* important and inspiring to do in life. One district bank manager imagined herself as an entrepreneur, doing work related to the church and family. A managing partner of a large international consulting firm imagined himself buying houses, fixing them up, and reselling them. A businesswoman imagined herself in a writer's studio working on a series of novels.

What holds us back from our dreams? Most people convince themselves that doing what they really want can never earn them money. We keep our dreams as lovely fantasies, never giving any thought to how we might implement them in our lives.

Another reason we don't pursue our dreams is that we often don't have the courage to try. We may be so afraid of failure we don't define our dreams or know how we would even begin to reach for them. It takes a lot of courage to do something significant and meaningful.

In this exercise, you will define your dreams without consideration for money, failure, or time of life. You have the time to attend medical school, get a law degree, or become a world-class stockbroker. This exercise differs from the "Today I am..." Visualization, in which the goal was to generate a range of common themes and values. Here you will be defining in concrete detail the elements and activities you need to create your ideal work situation.

Before you begin, take some time to practice the following visualizations. Read through each one and choose the one you like best—or use them both. They will help you think about your dream in minute detail. The clearer and more concrete you are about your dreams, the better.

You may want to read these visualizations aloud into a tape recorder and then lie down in a comfortable place, close your eyes, and listen to the recording. Have your notebook and a pen or pencil nearby so that afterward you can write down what you experienced.

Visualization 1: Finding Meaningful Work

Take a moment to make sure you are as comfortable as possible. (Pause). Good. Imagine that your ears are tiny microphones focusing in on the sounds of my voice. Any outside sounds simply enable you to become more relaxed.

Start noticing the natural rhythm of your breath as you breathe in and out. Let it happen naturally. At the count of three, I will ask you to take a nice deep breath. Imagine you are inhaling a color that symbolizes relaxation for you. Ready, one, two, three.

Let the color start flowing like a river through your body. It is relaxing all your muscles, nerves, and nerve endings. Starting at the top of your head, gently massaging your scalp and flowing down onto your face, smoothing away any sign of tension there and around the tiny muscles of your eyes and eyelids.

As this relaxation flows down your face, you may notice that your jaw wants to drop open. If it does, just let it. Let the color of relaxation flow down the back of your neck and into your shoulders. You may want to imagine that you are just like a rag doll, so loose and limp. Relaxation is flowing down like a river into your arms and hands. Let this breath of color flow into your chest and abdomen leaving you relaxed as you let this color penetrate the muscles in your abdomen and back, letting any sign of tension drain away. Just like a rag doll, so relaxed, knowing that the surface you are sitting on will support you. Now let this relaxation flow down into your buttocks and thighs, letting the tension melt away like butter melting in the noonday sun. Relax down into your calves and ankles and into your feet. Massaging your arches, toes, and nerve endings, down into the center of the earth and down a little bit more. If at any time unnecessary thoughts come to mind, imagine they are words written in the clouds being blown away by gentle breezes.

Now let's walk down a country path. Count the steps, from five to zero. You may feel a little more relaxed with each step. As you step down to five, notice the sights around you, the brightly colored flowers. Perhaps you see some trees and friendly animals. What sounds do you hear? Maybe birds chirping or the sound of leaves beneath your feet. Down to four then three, as you notice the temperature of the air, or perhaps a balmy breeze. Down to two and one. Being more relaxed, letting go just a little more, as you find a door in front of you.

Open the door to your private place; notice now what the door looks like. The texture and size, what shape and color. If it is locked, take out a key and unlock it. Go within and lock it behind you.

Now let your imagination flow freely as you create this private setting exactly as you'd like your ideal work space and setting to be: What are you wearing? Who is with you? What are you feeling and thinking? What are you doing? See yourself doing what you like to do. Make the scene peaceful, serene, happy, comfortable. In this moment of silence see or sense it now.

See yourself achieving the goal you want. Let all your senses come into play: sight, hearing, touch, smell, emotions. What is the quality of experience you want in your life? Imagine your goal in every detail. What is your attitude about yourself, your life, knowing you can attain any goal you set out to do. Take a moment to envision this in every detail.

Now take this successful you someplace exciting. Take this new self-image there now. See yourself and sense yourself in every detail. See people congratulating you on your success, see your sense of pride, accepting this as the real you.

Now let a warm glow of satisfaction permeate your body. You can say to yourself, I am this, I deserve this, I accept this. See or sense yourself doing your visualization each day. This is bringing you one step closer to your goal each time you do it.

See yourself setting aside fifteen minutes each day to visualize your ideal situation so you can achieve your goals. Knowing that setting aside time for visualizations each day is like an artist's brushstroke toward the completion of the painting. Now give thanks for all that you have and are about to receive.

It is time to leave your private place knowing you can easily return—just by relaxing and creating it in your mind.

Take a moment to say goodbye and close and lock the door behind you as you walk back up the steps and I will count from one to five.

With each step you will feel more alert, awake, and will be able to go to sleep when you decide to. Deep breath, one; two, more alert; three, objective state; four, coming back; five, alert and knowing you can go to sleep whenever you decide to. Back refreshed and alert.

After you sit up, take up your notebook or paper and crayons and write or *draw what you visualized. Use words, colors, and suggestions of images that you saw.*

Visualization 2: Finding Meaningful Work

Lie down on the floor. Get comfortable. Take a few deep breaths. Relax, uncross your arms and legs. Do not prop your head up, but lie so all parts of your body are level.

Hear the sound of the sea and birds. Listen to the sounds of the waves. Hear the sound of the surging and churning of water. There is a moment of silence as each wave flows out again to rejoin the ocean. Each wave, like each breath, is a reminder to look within. Each wave is like a rising and falling of each breath we take. Breath enters and releases. A silent awareness within that there is nowhere to go, nowhere to go.

All concerns for the world outside fade as you experience the calm that is yours now. A sense of floating on sound. Each sound reminds you that you are in a safe place. It reminds you that you can relax, deeply relax, and trust this process of life to take care of you. You may be noting the things that are surrounding you, your body, the air, clothing, the surface beneath you. You may be feeling the weight of your body pressing down as if you are lying gently relaxing in a hammock or cradled in salt water.

Let yourself sink deeply into the softness that rises up to contain you— sinking into those sensations. Gradually lose interest in things and events outside, soothed by the pleasant feelings of your skin. Be like a soft silken blanket. Let yourself begin to let go even more. Notice your closed eyelids, covering your eyes with a curtain of soft, moist, dark peace. Be aware now of the gentle rhythm and rise and fall of your chest or stomach with each breath.

Taking deep breaths in and letting air out. Feeling your body releasing the air. Taking another deep breath in—just experiencing it. Letting go as it makes space for the next breath. Now letting the breathing happen all by itself as if the air is breathing you. Feeling the chest and abdomen rise. Let all feelings of tension flow from your body and erase all previous thoughts and worries from your mind. Imagine that you are getting up on a wonderful day, one to five years from now. You have found your gifts and meaningful work.

You are sitting on the side of your bed trying to decide what kind of clothes you are going to wear. Take a moment and look over your wardrobe. What type of clothing do you finally decide to wear?

Imagine yourself getting ready to fill your day with meaningful work. What are your thoughts about the day to come while you are getting ready? What kind of feelings do you have as you look forward to your day? What gives you these feelings?

It's time for breakfast now. Are you sharing breakfast with someone or eating alone? After breakfast now, you are headed out the door. Stop for a moment and look around your neighborhood. What does it look like? What does your home look like? What thoughts and feelings do you experience as you look around?

Imagine now you're headed for work. How are you getting there? How far from home is it? What new feelings or thoughts are you experiencing?

You're entering your work situation now. Pause for a moment to get a mental picture of it. Think about where it is and what it looks like. Will you be spending most of your time indoors or outdoors? How many people will you be working with?

You are going to your specific job now. Who is the first person you encounter? What does he or she look like? What is he or she wearing? What do you say to him or her?

Try to form an image of the particular tasks you perform in your fulfilling, satisfying work. Don't think about it as a specific job with a title such as gardener or manager. Instead, think about what you are actually doing. Are you working with your hands, adding figures, writing, thinking, talking to people, or typing?

In your fulfilling work do you do it primarily by yourself or do you do it mostly with others? In your work with others, what do you do with them? How old are they? What do they look like? How do you feel toward them?

Where will you be going for lunch? Will you be going with someone else? Who? What will you be talking about?

How do the afternoon's activities differ from those in the morning? How are you feeling as the day progresses?

Your satisfying day is coming to an end now. Has it been a fulfilling day? If so, what made it that way? What about the day are you not satisfied with? Will you change these things?

Notice your breathing again. Your entire body expanding slightly with each breath letting go.

Notice your consciousness, your awareness is like your breathing. Your thoughts and feelings become filled with each thought and then it is time to let go and make space for the next awareness. Observe.

Now observe your breathing. Feel your limbs once again. When I count to three, you will return to this room.
One—saying goodbye to your fulfilling day of meaningful work.
Two—returning to this room, now.
Three—opening your eyes, returning relaxed and fully present.
Four—ready to find your true work.

Once again, remember the words and images you saw and draw or write down what you experienced. Try to be as specific and concrete as possible. Describe elusive images with adjectives, and describe what they looked like.

Applications to the Free-to-Succeed Society

These exercises allow you to name these ideal situations in concrete terms, so that they become recognizable, taking on form and depth.

After practicing these visualizations, Lily was able to write out the following application to the Free to Succeed Foundation:

If time and money were no object, I'd travel to new places with historical interest or interesting sociology. I'd return to school—study literature, history, archaeology, psychology. I'd find ways to work with people in the field of substance abuse. I'd significantly improve my commitment to exercise and health. I'd buy a house on a hill overlooking the ocean. I'd become an expert on wines. I'd go skiing every winter—all season at different resorts. I'd start my own business. I'd go dancing every night.

Now, write out your own heartfelt dream for application to the Free-to-Succeed Foundation. (The check will be arriving soon.)

The Pie of My Life Chart

Take a sheet of paper and draw a big circle that fills the page. Now take all the central themes that you have gleaned from the work in this chapter and draw pie slices representing the way in which you would divide your ideal day if time and money were no object. Debra made four equal slices in which work, family, gardening and solitude, and travel represented one-fourth each. Others broke their time down into finer slices. When done, compare this ideal day to what you have now. In what ways do they differ? What needs to be changed to bring your ideal day closer?

A Reunion Party

Once you are able to visualize what you want, you are more able to select the situations in your life that will lead you to your dream. Over time, your life can incorporate more and more elements of your dream until it becomes a reality.

I invite you to make believe that it is five years from now. You have discovered the notebook in which you put all your free-to-succeed information. You invite your friends over for a gathering. The conversation turns to a discussion on how far you have come in the five years. Listen to the way Lily described her previous five years:

"Since I saw you last, I bought a house in the Sonoma hills overlooking the ocean, and I even have a cellar for my wine collection. My health has improved considerably and I ski all winter near a place I own in Breckenridge, Colorado. I've returned to school and I am just about to get my master's degree in psychology. Meanwhile, I am doing an internship with battered women in my area."

You can choose to write a brief description of the changes you would like to have made five years from now, as Lily did. Or, you may take this exercise further and actually invite your friends to join in the fun. Invite them to a "five years from today" party and explain the "rules" of the game: that they should come as they hope to be in five years, ready to talk about the changes they have made, the relationships they have, and the goals they have accomplished. Ask them to bring the books they will have written, the portfolio they will have assembled, or floor plans for the house they will soon be completing.

Statement of Affirmation

After all these daydreams, probably one or two exciting ideas have formed in your mind. Write down a statement of affirmation about what you intend to do—maybe not just now, but soon. Complete the sentence, "I intend to..."

Here is Lily's statement of affirmation from all her visualizations: *I intend to become a psychologist and establish my own consulting business. I want to work with companies educating their employee assistance people on substance abuse.*

CAREER AEROBICS: WARM-DOWN PHASE

This is the last phase of the career aerobic process. Having stretched your creativity, we are preparing now to return to the real world. The adult self, that critic part of you, is probably anxiously waiting to be heard. The real-life obstacles to your dreams begin to loom.

Obstacles and How to Overcome Them

Visualize a garden, green and lush. Then visualize a wall. You can make it any size and shape. Imagine the texture, color, and height of the wall. On the other side, someone or something is waiting for you. How will you get over the wall? What is on the other side?

On one side of a piece of paper, list all the obstacles you can think of to finding your ideal situation. Go as long as you can, listing as many obstacles as you can.

Here is how Lily began her list:

Obstacles to my objective of establishing my own consulting firm:
1. Insufficient income during start-up phase.
2. No clients.
3. No long-term security.
4. Lack of structure—requires self-discipline.

5.   No community or support network.
6.   Fear of failure.

On the other side of the page she listed plans to overcome each obstacle:
1.   I can save money each month. I can take out a loan. I can get a loan on my house.
2.   I can talk to my existing clients at work and see if they want to come along with me.
3.   Job security is really an illusion anyway.
4.   I could organize my day just as I do at the job I now hold. I could rent an office so I will be away from the distractions of my house.
5.   I could attend professional conferences and lunches with colleagues so I get support and avoid feeling isolated.
6.   I could start seeing my therapist again if the fear of failure gets really bad.

Of course, Lily's list was much longer and filled with many more brainstorming ideas for each obstacle and how she planned to overcome it. Looking over her list, you'll see that some obstacles are grounded in reality, but others are grounded in irrational fear. It is important to identify these irrational self-imposed barriers for what they are. This is why I devised the Star and Dog exercise.

The Star and the Dog

As we get close to what we really want, we often find that two parts of ourselves are at odds with each other. There is the dreamer, the believer, who can envision the most extraordinary things for you, and the worrywart part of you. One side is the star and the other is the dog. They parallel the child, who imagines, and the adult, who worries. These two halves must strike a deal and come to some agreement in order to get you what you want. Here's how to do it.

First, identify the familiar parts that are in conflict and give each a name. Since they are polar opposites, use an oxymoron, a contradictory figure of speech that describes two mutually exclusive qualities: striving couch potato, contented nervous wreck, complacent opportunist, gentle warrior, or the security-conscious freedom-seeker.

Now, imagine a dialogue between the two. Write out what each would say to the other. Have each ask how they serve the other, what each appreciates and resents, and what each needs from the other.

Lily identified her star as a cocky, extremely self-confident know-it-all. A self-proclaimed expert. Her dog saw her as an impostor who feared others would think of her as a fraud and never call back. So when I asked Lily to identify her two contradictory selves, she said she was an incompetent expert.

Lily's Dialogue: The Incompetent Expert

Expert: It's depressing to see you again so soon. Can't you just go away and let me start my new glorious business?

Incompetent: I'm afraid that you'll fail. I don't think you know what you are doing.

Expert: I won't fail. In fact, I wish you would stop being such a sniveling mess. You make me ashamed.

Incompetent: I just want your attention. You need a plan. You need to listen to me. You can't just leap into this venture without some careful calculations and timetables.

Expert: I know that. Why do you keep bothering me?

Incompetent: Because you won't listen to me. I wish you'd stop criticizing me. I need reassurance that you'll be successful.

Expert: I guess I could be more compassionate and patient with you and reassure you. I guess I am too hard on you. I always feel like you are holding me back. Maybe I tend to leap before I look. I guess you could help me be more cautious, and I could be more patient and loving toward you.

Incompetent: I'd really love it if you treated me better. When I am frightened, just reassure me, then I wouldn't be so whiny all the time.

Expert: Okay, I guess I need to remember that we are in this together.

In this way, Lily was able to strike a deal with the two parts of her, especially the part that was holding her back from trying something new.

WHAT DOES ALL OF THIS MEAN?

Through Career Aerobics, you can begin to find ways to let your childlike self enter into your search for a crisis-proof career. In doing this, you have begun to see one or more directions out of your comfort zone and its survival patterns (which are primarily fixated on the result) and into the creative, inspired part of yourself.

If you have been persistent in these exercises, the childlike part in you is probably feeling more cooperative. The adult, too, may see your situation in a new light. To get what you want, to feel good about your choices, the child and the adult parts of yourself need to find a way of developing a productive relationship with one another. Like true partners, they need to find a way of respecting each other and recognizing how they can help each other. Only then can you be free to not only dream, but to make that dream a reality.

CHAPTER 6

LIVING BY YOUR OWN AGENDA
BUILDING A CRISIS-PROOF PLAN

*T*his is a test," read the sign on the copy room wall. "Repeat. This is only a test. Had this been your real life, you would have been shown where to go and what to do."

Like all such anonymous humorous signs, this one had a ring of truth to it. If only we knew the rules, we tell ourselves, we would know what to do in life. We could act and accomplish great things. Instead, we are left to make up the rules as we go along. From time to time, this sense of not knowing, of not having a clear-cut plan of action, overwhelms us.

My midthirties was such a time in my life. Fortunately, I had a friend who shared my situation. My upstairs neighbor Sue was an aspiring writer. After a morning of teaching and an afternoon of writing, Sue would come down for a cup of tea. Jokingly she would say, "I feel as if I'm never in the right place doing the right things. You know, never writing the right books, making the right plans, or negotiating the right salary."

"Or wearing the right clothes," I would chime in, "dating the right men, thinking the right thoughts, or pursuing the right career."

We would continue taking turns until the hilarity of it all sent us into fits of laughter. At the same time, it seemed so sadly true. We were never in the right place at the right time, doing the right things. Overwhelmed with the unmanageability of it all, we didn't have a clue as to where we were going. We just couldn't seem to wrap our arms around what we needed to feel satisfied with our lives.

Most of the people I've worked with have experienced similar feelings at one time or another—especially about their careers. They may even know what they want and where they would like to be, but they just can't seem to get focused with a plan that will take them there. Yet without one, they may never be able to find the fulfillment and satisfaction they hope for in life. The goal, then, is to create such a plan—one that is loose enough for providence to intervene and tight enough to keep them on course month by month.

This is the purpose of a crisis-proof career plan. Here you identify your career goal and the steps you will take to achieve it. Your plan resolves your uncertainties about your career and accommodates your need for both risk-taking and security.

The biggest impediment people face in creating a workable career plan is fear. A plan represents a commitment to new opportunities, new ways of being, and new horizons. All of us naturally cling to our comfort zone rather than face this brave new world. For better or worse (usually worse) we find our old selves reassuring, no matter how poorly they may fit us after ten, twenty, or thirty years. It is harder to act on our own uniqueness and to have the courage to assert who we really are than to stay with who we imagined ourselves to be, or whom our loved ones wanted us to be. Yet by articulating our dreams and seeing how we can realize them step by step, we can find the capacity to accept our uniqueness. This also means we can stop looking for acceptance in the external world and discover that we can provide it for ourselves.

A crisis-proof plan allows you to re-invent the rules of the game so you come out the winner. If you have completed the assessments in the previous chapters, your notebook is filled with invaluable information about yourself, where you are in your career, potential areas for growth, and what you need in your life for happiness, satisfaction, and fulfillment. Looking through these answers, you should have a sense of where you stand and some idea of where you want to go. In this chapter, you will assemble and integrate this information to create a life plan that has personal meaning and significance. By the end of this chapter, you will hold the blueprint for your own crisis-proof career.

WHAT MAKES THIS PLAN CRISIS-PROOF?

On a day-by-day basis, your crisis-proof plan gives you control over your life. You can pick up the plan on Monday and know exactly what you must do that day to take the next step toward your goal. At a time when you may be floundering, it gives you something concrete to hold on to. It helps you identify and use multiple resources to fuel your efforts. Each step helps you regain your confidence and self-worth.

On a deeper level, your crisis-proof plan gives you an understanding of yourself and options for the future that you might otherwise never have. Although your answers may change over time as your needs change, you will never again be left vulnerable to external changes in your job situation; whatever happens, you can brainstorm and put together a viable plan to see you through. And you need never risk endangerment due to internal changes occurring in your personal needs and attitudes about your work. Having once achieved this level of personal honesty, you will not be able to fool yourself into an endangered career again.

This chapter will guide you in building your plan for the short term and the long term. Before settling down to work, however, I suggest that you read through the entire chapter. I have included examples of others' plans and how they used their answers to the assessment tools in the previous chapters to form their crisis-proof plans. You can use these examples as guidelines when building your own plan.

Each of the three individuals whose story is told here has a different objective: Josie, currently employed, wants to escape from a precarious situation in a large corporation and begin a new career. Doug, suddenly laid off from his job, wants to find similar, more challenging work closer to home. And Ruth, a victim of corporate cutbacks, wants to stay where she is but reduce the stress in her life by using different skills. Whether your goal resembles one of these or is completely different, I will show you how to lay out a plan that will take you where you want to go.

PLAN A AND PLAN B: HOW TO USE EACH PLAN

A crisis-proof plan is made up of Plan A and Plan B. Think of Plan A as your *primary* plan. It is your ideal career, your first choice. It is a combination of the skills you want to use and the ideal job you described. It is a dream built on a sturdy foundation of common sense, capital, and planning. In building the plan you will develop short-term and long-term strategies to reach your career goal.

Plan B is your fallback plan, the safety net for your Plan A. If needed, it will serve as a temporary life-support system to see you through until you can make Plan A a reality. It allows you to take risks and to reach as far as you need to in Plan A, knowing that Plan B is there to help you survive in the interim.

People familiar with finance and investing will recognize the same elements in career planning. The variables are short- and long-term time frames and the degree of risk you are willing to take: low, moderate, or high. Plan A is typically a long-term venture with a relatively high degree of risk. Plan B is typically a short- or intermediate-term venture with relatively low risk.

Let's say your Plan A is to start your own business as a software developer and manufacturer. You have a great idea for a product. You have enough savings for a year. For the first six months you work to develop a product prototype on paper, get a programmer and manufacturer to develop the prototype, and find a market. After six months, however, you see that your savings won't cover living expenses and get the product out, too. So you jump to your fallback plan, Plan B, which is to take a job as a software engineer. Since it takes you four months to find this job, you have reinstated your income two months before your savings would have run out. You are not happy with the compromise, but you can continue to develop your product and budget your money until you can launch your Plan A again.

Some clients find that they must revise their plans as they get more information. People and situations change. Keep your plan flexible enough to revise and update it from time to time based on what you discover in the real world. On the other hand, don't make it so loose that it fails to give you the structure and discipline you need.

Robert's situation was typical. His career goal was to found and run a pharmaceutical company. He got off to a good start, but hit a snag in his Plan A and had to activate Plan B. Soon he was back to Plan A, only to encounter another obstacle. Back to Plan B. In fact, he did this three times in all. Robert didn't give up, however. Each time Plan A failed, he learned something new so he could try again. He finally got it right. Today he is very happy in his role as president of his own pharmaceutical company.

Take heart. Developing and following your crisis-proof career may seem an overwhelming task. Yet if you keep moving in the direction your plan indicates, your efforts will be rewarded. Opportunities will seem to emerge out of nowhere. It may be hard to believe that they are all part of your effort and intention, but they are.

HOW TO PUT TOGETHER YOUR PLAN

You will form your plan out of your answers to the self-assessment tools and exercises in chapters 2 through 5. You will summarize these answers into a coherent progression from which you will then map out your Plan A and Plan B. To do this, you will take the pages from your loose-leaf notebook(s) and assemble them as indicated in the following directions. The four questions of chapter 3 will provide the general framework:

Who am I?
What are my skills, gifts, and talents?
Where do I want to make (or continue to make) a contribution?
What trade-offs must I make?

Who Am I?

Your answers to this question have to do with the events, people, and experiences in your life that made you who you are today.

MARKETABILITY/STRESS • (Questions 1–5)

Materials to Assemble:

How Marketable Are You, Anyway?
Your Marketable Personality Skills
The Complete Job Burnout Scale

To help you summarize your answers from the above assessments, answer the following questions on a clean piece of paper in your notebook. Answer each question thoroughly, but be as concise as possible.

1. In assessing my external marketability, what are my most vulnerable areas?
2. What are my areas of strength in terms of my external marketability?
3. In assessing my marketability based on my personality, what are my vulnerable areas?
4. What are my areas of strength in terms of my personality?
5. What is my present stress level—low, moderate, or high?
   • What plans can I (or have I) formulated to reduce the stress (e.g., exercise program, more sleep, more time off)?

Balance • (Question 6)

This section summarizes the different areas of your life. When in balance, they nourish and enhance one another: for example, a good relationship at home gives you the emotional strength to meet new challenges at work. If out of balance, one area can impinge on your performance in other areas.

Materials to Assemble:

Someone I Admire/Someone I Envy
Postcards From the Other Side
The Question-and-Answer Game₁
Rewriting My Childhood Story
The Pie of My Life Chart
The Satisfaction Indicator

6. Where is my life currently most out of balance?
   ▪ What people, events, and experiences do I need to decrease in my life?
   ▪ What people, events, and experiences do I need to increase in my life?
   ▪ What do I want to add to my life that is not mentioned above?

Values ▪ (Question 7)

Materials to Assemble:

The Values Indicator
Today I Am...
The Satisfaction Indicator

7. What are my most important values?
   ▪ What are my top five values?
   ▪ To what extent are they reflected in my current job?
   ▪ On a day-to-day basis, am I acting from what I say are my most important values?
   ▪ Are my values at odds with my behavior, my job, and/or what I do?
   ▪ If so, how do I plan to reconcile them?

Financial Situation ▪ (Question 8)

Working six to eight hours a day, it generally takes a good three to six months to find another job in the same career, six to eight months to make a career change, and twelve months to start your own service business—longer for a product-oriented business.

8. In light of these facts, what is my financial situation?

What Are My Skills, Gifts, and Talents?

This section summarizes the activities you like to do and areas of interest you want to learn more about. It will help you develop a job description that incorporates the skills you find challenging and wish to develop.

Key Job Factors ▪ **(Question 9)**

Materials to Assemble:

> Find Your Bliss Grid
> Critical Job Factors Assessment
> Double Checklist of Job Likes and Dislikes

9. What do I want the work content of my job to be?
    ▪ What are the five key ingredients that make up a satisfying job situation, where I can perform my best (in order of importance)?

Ideal Job/Ideal Career ▪ **(Questions 10–17)**

Materials to Assemble:

> My Next Ideal Career Situation
> The Ideal Want Ad
> The Free-to-Succeed Society
> A Reunion Party
> Statement of Affirmation

10. What is my ideal job?
11. Does my description reflect the five key factors listed under question 9? If not, rewrite it to include these factors.
12. What would my ideal want ad say?
13. If time and money were not an issue and success were guaranteed, what would I be doing in my career?
14. What would my ideal workday be, including specifics about who, what, where, and when?
     ▪ What would my ideal career be?
15. What elements do I need that I do not have now? (Make a summary and composite picture of your ideal career, being as specific and concrete as possible. Don't just say, "I want to work with people"—say what kind of people: preschool-age children, executives, volunteers, etc.)
     ▪ Is there a discrepancy between my ideal day and my answers to question 13?
     ▪ What is the discrepancy?

- Is it a difference between earning a living and working at what I enjoy? If so, this difference may outline a plan that will take you to your goal. For example, if my ideal job is working as the controller of a small company, and my fantasy is being an entrepreneur with the autonomy to spend more time with my kids, I have the makings of a plan: I have a short-term goal (being a controller) and a long-term goal (being an entrepreneur). Now all I have to do is to fill in the gaps and look for sequential linkages. From this I can establish the action steps that will get me first to the one goal and then to the second.

16. How would I describe the changes I want to have made in my life one year from now (or five years from now), as I did in A Reunion Party?

17. How can I rewrite my Affirmation Statement to reflect my career goal?

Where Do I Want to Make (or Continue to Make) a Contribution?

This section summarizes the "where" of your plan. Where do you want to put down roots, live, commute, build your complex, or lease your office? (You may have included this information in previous questions. If so, skip it here.)

Optimum Environment • (Question 18)

Materials to Assemble:

Critical Job Factors Assessment (specifically, working conditions, job content, location/travel/commute)

18. Where do I perform my best?
   - What factors can't I live without?

What Trade-offs Must I Make?

This section summarizes the risks you are willing to take and what you are willing to sacrifice to gain the career goal you really want.

Choices and Obstacles ▪ **(Questions 19–22)**

Materials to Assemble:

Career Lifeline

Obstacles and How to Overcome Them

19.   What choices did I make early in my career that led me to where I am today?

20.   What did I learn from these choices?

21.   What obstacles are in the way of my current choices?

   ▪ What are all the obstacles that I perceive internally and externally that are keeping me from what I want?

22.   What are the strategies I will use to overcome the obstacles? Use this format: First list the obstacle, the goal you are striving for, and then the strategies. For example:

   Obstacle: My career goal involves using a computer and I don't have any knowledge of computers at all.

   Goal: To learn basic computer skills.

   Strategies:

   1. Take an adult education course on computers at the local junior college.

   2. Call my sister and ask her to let me practice on her computer.

   3. Ask my friends who have computers what they like about theirs and what they would recommend.

The answers to these twenty-two questions comprise the basic information you will need to draft your crisis-proof plan. This information may change with time, but for now, you know your marketability, your level of stress, the areas that are out of balance in your life, your most important values, your financial situation, your ideal job, and so on.

THE ANATOMY OF A PLAN

Your Plan A will be made up of several specific components as described below. In addition, it will answer the following question:

What is my career goal? A goal is a statement that is concrete, specific, and measurable. Whether it is to start your own business or to be CEO of the company for which you now work, your goal is the yardstick against which to measure your progress and to keep you on track. The rest of Plan A is a blow-by-blow description of how you are going to achieve that goal.

For example, "My goal is to start my own business in health-care consulting by June of next year." "My goal is to become the vice-president of this company in five years." "My goal is to write a book about executive development coaching by autumn of next year. This book will launch my career as a consultant and coach. I will use it as a marketing tool to start my own consulting business."

Remember that in order to actualize your career goals, you must feel they are your own. If they are important only to please someone else and not yourself, you will probably find excuses for not working toward them. You can waste a lot of valuable effort and time halfheartedly pursuing other people's goals.

What Is My Plan A?

Your Plan A will have at least one career goal and one long-term strategy. Your long-term strategy includes what you plan to do by the end of this month, the end of the quarter, the end of this year and next year, and in the years to come until you achieve your goal. If your plan involves a number of years, you may decide to divide your action steps, resources, and time lines into one-year intervals.

Some plans may also have a short-term goal and a short-term strategy. Many long-term career goals, particularly if they involve a major change in your career, require one or more interim steps. For example, to become a lawyer, you first need to obtain a law degree and pass the bar. Or you may need to qualify for a major real estate loan before you can buy the land for your ranch in Montana.

Your short-term strategy is what you plan to do today, this week, and this month to take you to your short-term goal and eventually to your long-term goal.

What Is My Plan B?

Plan B is your safety net, your security plan. Since it involves skills you already know and have used to earn a living in the past, Plan B typically is short-term and requires little risk. You will build it from the first two boxes of the Find Your Bliss Grid: "Things I never want to do again" and "Things people say I do well, but I take for granted."

Many people in their eagerness to reach their ideal career want to skip Plan B or give it little consideration. This is understandable, but often impractical.If you have only a month's savings to see you to your Plan A, for example, you need to reframe Plan B and make it part of your strategy to reach Plan A.

If you are in a more fortunate position, you still need a Plan B. Be realistic in your assessment of how long you can afford to work on Plan A with your current financial situation.

Both Plan A and Plan B include action steps, resources, and time lines.

- *Action steps* are activities you must undertake to implement your plan.
- *Resources* include the specific information, people, and materials you need to draw on to accomplish those action steps. Your resources might include lists of target businesses, books on certain subjects, network referrals, and so forth.
- *Time lines* give you the deadlines and sense of progress that will structure your efforts. When you see your plan broken down day by day, week by week, into manageable increments, you can see how the impossible becomes possible.

It is important to remember that no two career goals are the same. Some people think in big visions—ten to twenty years down the line—while others think three and five years ahead. Still others think in what I call baby visions—they follow their curiosities day by day. Each curiosity they explore leads them to the next opportunity.

Patricia had an entry-level position as an editorial assistant in a small cookbook company. Eager to work in publishing and develop her editorial skills, she took on all the free-lance work that came her way: sales brochures, magazine articles, and cookware pamphlets. Without consciously planning an overall career strategy, Patricia consistently moved in her chosen direction, one curiosity at a time. Ten years later, she had her own free-lance business and worked on a daily basis with authors, agents, and publishers.

WRITING YOUR OWN AGENDA: YOUR CAREER GOAL AND PLAN A AND PLAN B
Following the example given below, prepare a sheet of paper (or a

computer file) on which to write out your Plan A and then your Plan B.

PLAN A

My Career Goal:

Action Steps   **Resources**   **Time Line**

My Short-term Goal:

Action Steps   **Resources**   **Time Line**

PLAN B

Goal:

Action Steps	Resources	Time Line

Helpful Guidelines

As you construct your Plan A and Plan B, here are some useful guidelines to keep in mind.

Don't be afraid to write out your plan as many times as you need to until it seems right. If you have several ideas, write them all out and see which one seems best. Setting down your plans on paper takes you a step further than just deciding on a career goal and talking about it with others. It constitutes a deeper commitment to yourself. Also, seeing it on paper makes it more concrete. You and others can more readily assess the plan's merits and failings. In this form, you can show it to friends and confidants and ask for advice and ideas.

The more specific and detailed you are in writing your plan, the better. But remember, any plan is just an approximation of the future. We can't really know what life has in store for us, so be prepared to adjust your plan as time goes on and situations change.

Don't think too small. Don't think in terms of just earning a living. Think creatively of the ways in which you can leverage your skills into a career that holds more interest and satisfaction for you. Even in your Plan B, you can probably discover new, more satisfying ways to combine old skills.

Janis is a group controller for a large semiconductor company. The money is good, but she has little interest in the company's product. She imagines working as the CEO for a smaller company that would allow her to connect her work life to something personally meaningful. She loves gardening, entertaining, and taking care of her family. She has targeted twenty-five small and medium-size companies related to these interests: publishers of gardening and landscaping books, mail-order gardening-supply companies, expensive household furnishings manufacturers, a cookware company, and so on. In using her business skills in one of these companies, she will be able to find a professional challenge with personal meaning.

Don't get discouraged. A crisis-proof approach takes time and commitment. You'll need to demonstrate your commitment by choosing your goal and putting in the hours, the effort, and the energy before you can expect to see results.

You will be tested. If you are ambivalent about your plan, you will externalize your doubts. If you can't decide whether to start your own business or look for a job, you'll probably receive a job offer that falls short of your true goal. It will tempt you to settle for less than you set out to achieve. This dilemma is the way people create an external problem to work out while they work to resolve their inner confusion about what they really want to do. If this happens, return to your assessments and reread your answers to questions concerning your ideal career. Recommit to your goal and keep yourself from being sidetracked.

Several ideas may be better than one. Let's say you have five ideas and they all seem equally attractive. Write them out in sequence according to what you want to do first, then the next, and the next. Now sit back and brainstorm as to how they might fit together into one cohesive plan. If an integrating plan fails to appear, select the one or two ideas that fit together best and seem the most attractive to you. As you continue to work with the material, you will become more certain of your best choice.

PUTTING IT ALL TOGETHER: JOSIE JACOBSON CHANGES HER CAREER

Josie Jacobson has worked as a vice president in marketing at a consumer-products company for the last fifteen years. In the last several years, however, she's been noticing changes in the company and its attitudes.

"It's a subtle thing," she told me, "where you sense that people aren't being treated as well as they were in earlier years. Somewhere we turned a corner and became a big company. We have the same number of people, but we are trying to do a lot more.

"In the last four years, we've reorganized about every nine months. We've had two new presidents. Many of my old friends have gone, mostly through layoffs or voluntary programs. I don't understand how I have remained. Here I am, but I'm not happy anymore. People act paranoid all the time, hoping to hang on, but expecting the worst.

"Once again, we are going through a reorganization, but I'm tired of all the politics and I want out. They had me interview with the new boss in my new assignment. I've heard many awful things about him. If he doesn't like me, I'm sure I'll be asked to leave in the next round of layoffs. The job itself is basically a staff position. I don't have any bottom-line responsibility."

Many people, like Josie, see the handwriting on the wall; she recognized many of the critical warning signs in her situation and could guess what they meant. At my suggestion, Josie worked through the exercises in this book and then started to work on her crisis-proof career plan.

WHO AM I?

In assessing my external marketability, what are my most vulnerable areas? I am not living in a region with many consumer-product companies as competitors. So if I want to stay in the industry and go to a major competitor, I would have to relocate. With four children and a husband with a fairly secure job, I can't do that.

What are my areas of strength? I have contact with outside agencies. I live in a part of the country that is now just as recession-proof as other parts.

In assessing my marketability based on my personality, what are my vulnerable areas? I don't have a ten-year plan (yet). I never kept a black book, so tracing important contacts will take time and effort.

What are my areas of strength? I am aggressive and outgoing. I enjoy entertaining and meeting new people. I find cold calling a challenge and get more tenacious as the resistance increases.

What is my present stress level? High! I am off the charts. Frequently, I am so busy trying to prove myself that I keep taking on more and more, and I succeed exceptionally well. I stop setting limits because my boss will think I can't meet the challenge. This is how I gradually do myself in. (Corporations love workaholics like me.)

Where is my life currently most out of balance? Personal time! I need to get away. First, I need to forget that I am responsible for a bunch of kids, a husband, and a job. The only privacy I get is in the shower and driving in my car. Life used to be fun. I need some time alone to rediscover myself. At least that is how it feels now. Maybe I wouldn't have to escape to Tahiti indefinitely. Perhaps a weekend in Carmel might do just fine.

Then, if I stay with my job, I still have time off coming to me. The kids and I could escape to the cabin for two weeks—no phone, no television. Just hiking, reading, and roasting marshmallows.

What are my most important values? I want a job oriented more toward the social welfare of others. In my Today I Am exercise I enjoyed imagining my role in humanitarian projects and organizations, as well as doing things that were fun and pleasurable.

What is my financial situation? If I decide to leave right away, it would put a strain on our budget, just when we have decided to remodel the house. Financially, I'll be better off staying put. I hate to have to worry about money.

Doing these exercises helped Josie decide to take the staff job that was offered her. She came to this decision after a weekend alone in Carmel where she took long walks on the beach and thought about her career. She realized that she was too vulnerable now to make a big change. She decided to keep the stability of her job while she made important changes to improve her health and lower her level of stress.

I often recommend that clients take some time off, even if it's just a weekend out of town. People frequently find that the best thing they can do for themselves is change the scenery, however briefly. The break prepares you to forge ahead with a relaxed mind and see your choices more clearly.

Josie came back ready to continue work on her plan. Making the decision to stay freed her to move ahead more confidently. She was eager to get going on her crisis-proof plan and curious where it would take her. Here are highlights of her answers.

WHAT ARE MY SKILLS, GIFTS, AND TALENTS?

What do I want the work content of my job to be? I want to develop a business. I want to spend my day meeting clients, making presentations, developing creative ideas, and closing sales.

These are the seven key factors that make up a satisfying job situation for me. (Although Josie listed seven, you can list as many as you want, from five to ten.)
1. Better salary.
2. Some creative control over advertising and marketing strategies.
3. A commute of no more than thirty to forty-five minutes.
4. A financially stable employer with a reputation of treating people well and few layoffs.
5. Ethical company.
6. Coworkers with similar interests.
7. Company that makes a difference to people.

What is my ideal job? My ideal job is having my own consulting business. My short-term goal is to work in an ad agency that will give me the experience to start my own business. I want to work for an agency that has interesting clients and where I feel I can make a significant contribution.

When Josie compared her description of her ideal job to the critical job factors she had listed before, this is what she wrote:

The critical factor missing from my job description is a short commute time. I will plan to find an ad agency close enough to home that my commute is about half an hour each way.

My ideal want ad would read: Senior advertising person with fifteen years experience needed for small, prestigious agency. Service-business experience necessary. Skills include extensive client contact, creative ad campaigns, and 10 percent travel. Salary negotiable.

What would my ideal workday be? Josie compared her ideal day and her newspaper want ad with her answer to question 13 ("If time and money were not an issue..."). She wrote: I would have the freedom to work as much or as little as I wanted. I would own my own consulting business and have several large clients. I would contract out work that I didn't want to handle.

A reunion party: I'm so glad to be here. In the last year, I left my company and took a job in a small ad agency with really bright, creative people. The thing that I love about it is that we all have a lot of autonomy. That gives me time for other interests in my life. Any stress I feel is usually because I'm so stimulated by the work. I have a variety of clients and assignments, and my time is more under my control. I am still learning all I can to eventually start my own business.

Affirmation statement: I will find creative work at an ad agency so that I can leave my present job and gain the skills to start a company of my own.

WHERE DO I WANT TO MAKE (OR CONTINUE TO MAKE) A CONTRIBUTION?

Where do I perform my best? An environment with lots of windows and natural light, and trees outside. The work areas would be well suited both to individual and group projects (e.g., individual offices as well as a large group-meeting area). I want a commute that is forty-five minutes or less so I can have time for my family.

WHAT TRADE-OFFS MUST I MAKE?

What choices did I make early in my career that led me to where I am today? I realize that many of my early career choices were not well thought out. As long as I was moving ahead, I thought I was making progress. In one way, this was good for me because I gained experience with many different products. On the other hand, I wish I had paid more attention to the future.

Some earlier choices also closed some doors for me. I didn't go to college, so there are some career situations for which I am not qualified. Fortunately, at my age, I can expect to move ahead based on my track record.

What obstacles are in the way of my current choices? My obstacles:

1. I am not feeling very confident about leaving my job after all

these years. Maybe it's because I haven't looked for a job in such a long time—my fear of the unknown.

2. I feel an overwhelming sense of failure. I got as far as I could go. Maybe I don't have what it takes to get to the top.

3. My inability to "let go" of corporate life (I have a love/hate relationship). I feel responsible to people who work for me.

4. Concerns about financial security, both short- and long-term. I fear there is less financial security in what I am seeking.

5. Concerns about self-discipline. Will I really be able to work without a structure?

What are the strategies I will use to overcome the obstacles?

Obstacle: Lack of confidence.

Goal: To build more confidence.

Strategies:

1. Complete a personal motivation training seminar (by fall).

2. Become an active participant in a personal development group (by end of summer).

3. Look into short-term therapy with Dana's therapist. Get an appointment (by next week).

Obstacle: Feelings of failure.

Goal: To gain some perspective on the situation.

Strategies:

1. Daily accomplishment plan (by next week).

2. Daily exercise—renew gym membership (call tomorrow).

3. Reduce alcohol consumption: no more than two glasses of wine a week (starting now).

4. Get feedback from five people that I trust (by end of month).

Obstacle: Letting go of corporate life.

Goal: To feel less responsible and more dispensable.

Strategies:

1. Gradually reduce work schedule.

2. Take lunches to network at least three times a week (start end of month).

3. Subscribe to placement newsletter and clipping service from local graduate school (start in fall).

4. Find out when next professional association meeting is being held (by next week).

5. Develop effective self-managing teams at work (complete in two weeks).

Obstacle: Financial security.

Goal: To save some money, so I can move forward without anxiety.

Strategies:

1. Talk to Jack and ask him to help me develop a business plan for new business (by end of summer).

2. Develop a budget (by end of month).

3. Start an account to save money (by end of summer).

Obstacle: Self discipline.

Goal: To feel as if I am in control of my life and not a victim.

Strategies:

1. Develop effective healthy eating program and lose ten pounds. Ask at gym for program recommendation and referral to a nutritionist.

2. Work on career plan—one hour a day minimum.

Josie's Plan A

My career goal: To own and operate my own consulting business within three years time and make a profit. I want to have two people working for me either as employees or subcontractors.

Action Steps:

Achieve short-term goals. That is, get a job at an ad agency and learn the following: how to get clients, how to negotiate fees, how to generate return business or contracts, and how to create long-term relationships.

Take a sales training course to help me refresh my skills.

Leave and take a few client accounts with me. Negotiate with my employer so there will be no conflict of interest.

If all goes well, this plan will take about three years. If things don't go well, I have a fallback plan (Plan B) to stay at my present job or find a job with a competitor.

Resources:

A really ideal situation in a small ad agency from which I could build my plan.

Additional knowledge about financial management and the consulting industry in my area.

Stability at home (no more kids, my husband keeping his job for at least four years).

Saving some money as a financial cushion.

Planning a daily regimen to provide some structure, feedback, and support. I could use my office at home to make calls, outline my daily schedule to include lunches and networking, and take a course to sharpen up my writing skills.

Time line: Three years.

My Short-term goal: To work for a small ad agency within forty-five minutes of my home.

Action Steps:

Call the chambers of commerce in the three counties that are within forty-five minutes of my home. Get their directories of companies.

Ask friends for the names of firms they would recommend.

Resources:

Generate a list of people I've known in the past and present to talk to about my intentions.

Find time to meet with them during work hours.

Additional ads, recruiters, and placement services to uncover openings.

Time line: Three months at the minimum and five months at the maximum to take transition steps into smaller ad agency firm.

Josie's Plan B

Goal: I will continue to work for my old company or a smaller competitor, supplier, or vendor in consumer products.

Action steps:

Get a list of all competitors.

Work with the list until I find the one whose conditions meet at least two ingredients of my ideal job.

Implement sound marketing strategy.

Get names from colleagues of people they know who might help.

Go to regional and national professional conferences for networking.

Resources:

Friends' leads.

Lots of telephone calls.

A lot of effort.

Time at lunch and at end of day.

Talk to husband about my plans and keep him updated.

Time line: If I can't land a job in an advertising agency within four months, I'll start at once on this plan, hoping to find a job within three months.

Now came the hard part—doing it! It took several months, but Josie was successful in implementing her Plan A. The fact that she knew what she wanted allowed her to communicate it to others. She left her old company and worked at the ad agency for two years. Today she has her own consulting business. She even has two people working for her and several major corporate clients, just as she wanted. Josie stuck to her plan.

She came back to my office recently to visit. Like all those who find their bliss, Josie looked seasoned and radiant. When she talked about her career, she reminded me of the effort and energy it took to stick to her dream. "But it was worth it all," she said.

DOUG CORD WANTS MORE JOB FULFILLMENT

In contrast to Josie's, Doug's plan is very straightforward. He had only two key factors that he wanted to change, and not surprisingly, these appeared consistently in his assessments.

Doug was a design engineer in a chemical company for many years. He loved the engineering work, but after a reorganization, he began to question his loyalty and commitment to the firm.

I know from my own experience that many employees feel the same ambivalence about changes in their work environment. They wonder if they should just sit tight and see if they can ride out the storm. "Every day is like watching a soap opera, *As the Ax Falls*, around this company," reported Doug. "It's easier to stay put, I guess, than decide to leave on your own. It's hard to see the toll it takes on you in subtle ways. Your self-confidence and your health begin to erode."

One day, he, too, became a statistic. "I guess I breathed a sigh of relief when Maggie, the human resources person, brought me into her office and told me that my job and others like it were 'going away,' as she put it. I had not been happy at what I was seeing around me for a long time."

WHO AM I?

Doug got to work on the assessments. Here are some of his answers:

In assessing my external and internal marketability, what are my strengths/what are my weaknesses? I am highly marketable in my skills, education, and job location. I'm unaware of any significant weaknesses.

What's my stress level? Low. I'm not stressed out. In fact, I'm relieved and optimistic about the layoff.

Where is my life currently most out of balance? I want more time for my wife and daughter. I want to coach my daughter's soccer team in the afternoon. I want more time to go bicycle touring and racing with my friends.

What are my most important values? I want to do intellectually stimulating work. I want closer relationships with my family and closer relationships with my coworkers, as I used to have in my old company.

What's my financial situation? I'm in good shape; I can take a year off to look for just the right position, but I'd rather keep the money in an interest-earning account somewhere.

WHAT ARE MY SKILLS, GIFTS, AND TALENTS?

I like being an engineer. In my next job I would like to tackle thorny problems and do interesting work as a design engineer. I want to work closer to home so I have more time for the family.

The five key factors that make up a satisfying job situation, where I can perform at my best:

1. A five-minute commute. My present job is a ninety-minute commute. All I do now is commute, work, and sleep.

2. Stimulating work.
3. Time for my family.
4. Fifteen percent raise in salary.
5. Coworkers and senior management who enjoy their work and share my values.

What is my next ideal position? My ideal position is five minutes away from my home in a research and development division where there isn't so much job pressure. I want a job as a design engineer in a big company with my own office and interesting projects.

What would my newspaper ad say? Design engineer wanted for research and development division of large pharmaceutical company. Ten years experience in engineering. No travel, salary negotiable.

A reunion party: I am so glad to be part of this new organization. I love my work. My assignments are stimulating and so are the people. I can ride my bicycle to work and get home in time for my daughter's soccer game. I have a lot of joy in my work and my personal life.

Affirmation statement: I will find a company close to home with interesting engineering work.

WHERE DO I WANT TO MAKE (OR CONTINUE TO MAKE) A CONTRIBUTION?

Where do I perform my best? A research-oriented environment with a short commute (five minutes or less) from my home.

WHAT TRADE-OFFS MUST I MAKE?

What choices did I make early in my career that led me to where I am today? What did I learn from those choices? What I saw in my career lifeline is that I was so achievement oriented when I was younger that I sacrificed my first and second marriages. I also relied on alcohol to relax me after a hard day. Now I know more of what I want and won't let unbridled ambition take me over. I use exercise to relax in the evening, rather than alcohol.

What obstacles are in the way of my current choice? My obstacles:
1. I may not be able to find the right ingredients all in one job. I may just get desperate and take the first thing.

2. My skills in job search are very rusty.

How I plan to overcome the obstacles:

Obstacle: Not find the right ingredients all in one job

Goal: To hold out for the right job

Strategies:

1. I will tell my wife about my fears and ask her to help me.
2. I will ride my bicycle around the several industrial parks near my home and jot down the names of all the companies in them.
3. I will ask my friends if they know anyone I can talk to in those companies, so I can use them as references to get interviews.

Obstacle: My job search skills are rusty.

Goal: To sharpen my job search skills.

Strategies:

1. I will read as many books as possible on the subject.
2. I will talk to as many people as possible about search skills, what they know, what they find useful, etc.
3. I will practice interview role-playing with my sister, who is in human resources at a nearby company.

Doug's Plan A

My career goal: To find a job as a design engineer in a research company close to my home so I can ride my bicycle there each day and have time for my family at night.

Action steps: I will get on my bicycle and explore the neighborhood. I know I live near some medium-size industrial parks. I'll jot down the names of the companies. I'll develop a list of neighbors, friends, and former coworkers to contact and call my friends who have left my present company. I'll find out where they are and what they are doing and tell them of my plan; then ask for ideas, companies, and leads.

I will ask them to give me names of anyone they know who works in engineering in these companies. I'll keep doing that until I find some openings.

Resources:

I need to begin networking.

I need to get together a list of recruiters, friends, and professionals.

I need to get a list from the local chamber of commerce of all the companies that hire engineers in this area.

I need to put together my new resumé and cover letter to send out.

I need to put together a list of target companies.

Time line: In the next four months.

Doug's Plan B

After four months, I will take a job farther away from home.

Action steps: If nothing turns up after four months of implementing Plan A, I will start to answer ads and follow up leads for jobs farther away from my home.

Resources: Same as my ideal job, but for a different area.

Time line: If I cannot get Plan A to work after the first four months.

In the end, Doug's strategy paid off. By identifying nearby companies and networking, he found a job five minutes away from his home. He rides his bicycle to work each day. He works as a design engineer in the research division of a waste-management company.

Today, Doug has more time for his family. He uses the time he once spent commuting to coach his daughter Cassie's soccer team. Doug couldn't have found the job if he hadn't followed his plan.

WHAT KEEPS PEOPLE FROM THEIR PLAN

Josie and Doug are good examples of people who built their plans and followed them through step by step. They were able to make the transitions and changes they needed to accomplish what they really wanted to in their lives and their careers. Josie and Doug are representative of the majority of the people I work with. I hope that your experience will be similar.

A successful plan can be simple or complex. Whatever it is, remember that it must be designed for you and no one else. You need to lay it out in a way that is meaningful and productive for you.

A few individuals do not find a successful outcome or have more difficulty than Josie and Doug. Many people take the time to build their plan, only to be seduced back to their comfort zone and to lose sight of their commitment. The sad part is that they know they are sacrificing their dreams, but the illusion of security is so enticing they would rather stick out ten more years in a job that isn't challenging than think things through, develop a plan, and put in the effort to make their dream a reality. What they don't realize is the price they pay. When they settle for the limited horizons of their comfort zone, their self-esteem deteriorates and they become one of the endangered species.

Another mistake most people make is that they want it all to happen *now*. After years of drifting, taking whatever opportunities came their way, they somehow want to find the career equivalent to the proverbial get-rich-quick scheme. In one long-overdue move, they suddenly want the job and career of their dreams.

At thirty-five or forty-five, it is hard not to feel you've done your time. Why should you have to get more focused now? Haven't you paid your dues? The answer is no. So far, you've been lucky. Now is the time—before it is too late—to put together all you know about yourself and act on it. Luck may not intervene time after time.

A PLAN THAT FAILED: RUTH GAGE WANTS TO USE DIFFERENT SKILLS

Ruth Gage, a vice president and manager in a bank, called me just after her return from a four-week vacation.

"The last four weeks were wonderful! After the second week I felt happily brain-dead," she told me. "I've been back three days and I'm back in the soup! I'm just as stressed out as I was before I left, and I can't believe that it took only three days. I've got to do something different. Can I come in and talk things out?"

I told Ruth that she needed to put these feelings in perspective. Most people feel terrible the first week back, when the constraints of the very small box they have built for themselves are most noticeable. The first impulse is to get depressed and doubt yourself. Ruth assured me that she wasn't going to do anything impulsive. It had taken her many long and hard years to get where she was, and she wasn't going to jump ship now because of postvacation stress.

When we got together, she had gone through all the assessments. Here is what she wrote:

In assessing my external marketability, what areas are my most vulnerable? My company is in the more unstable area of the economy right now. I must realize that I am a victim of a larger problem. Our market share has declined recently. Our company has pared staff before, so it is likely they will do it again. I have assumed the work load of three other managers who have left, and my direct reports have increased from three to seven. I am now the manager of two hundred employees. There have been rumors that my company is going to be acquired by a Japanese firm. I have noticed that some of the current work projects in the other divisions are being farmed out to free-lance contractors.

(So far Ruth's vulnerability was alarmingly high. No wonder Ruth was experiencing extraordinary stress, despite the four-week vacation!)

In assessing my marketability based on my personality, what are my strengths? I am very marketable. Although I haven't been on an interview for many years, I think that I can handle myself with confidence. I consider myself an extrovert and I am tenacious. I am ready to take a greater risk, now that I am in my forties and feel more comfortable with myself, than when I first started working for the bank. I like to network with people.

Above all, I would like to try something new to stretch myself in the next year. I know it will be difficult, but I am willing to do it.

I have found these to be my most vulnerable areas in my marketability based on my personality: Like most people, I don't really have a clear vision of what I want to achieve. I don't have a career plan.

What's my stress level? High. I find it hard to bounce back. I feel like I am working harder and harder, and producing less and less. I feel old and ugly when I look in the mirror in the morning. Sometimes in a meeting, I just blank out and forget what I was going to say, or I forget a client's name during an important conversation. At home, I pour myself a martini and just forget about dinner. On the weekends, I often don't get out of my bathrobe and slippers.

At work, they just keep piling it on. You don't realize that it is happening because you want to perform well. Finally, you are hopelessly buried, but you are too tired to cry *Stop!* You worry that they will think you can't cut it. Everyone around you is arriving early and staying late. As the boss, you don't want to be the one to cave in first.

What parts of my life need to get in more balance? Work seems to occupy most of my time and is my overriding concern. I have little time to gain some perspective on my life. My husband and I are probably not as intimate as we once were because my attention is focused on work. I'm constantly worried that something will drop through the cracks.

What are my important values? My major values are helpfulness, friendship, and inner harmony. Before, when the business was smaller, I used to find these in my job. There was a sense of family there. Now that the business has grown and I'm in upper management, I no longer feel this. I'd like to spend more time in a less visible spot. I don't have the same desire to achieve and prove myself that I did in my earlier days.

What's my financial situation? I need to work. I have a big mortgage and debts. If I am extremely careful, I can live for six months without a job, but it would be a struggle.

What gifts and skills do I want to use? I'd like to use roughly the same gifts and skills, but in a less pressured setting.

The five key ingredients/job content that make up a satisfying job situation where I can perform my best are:

1. Fewer time pressures and deadlines.
2. A smaller team to manage.
3. A staff job that doesn't deal with the bottom line.
4. Educated, friendly, and professional staff.
5. Time to develop relationships with customers and clients.

Ruth realized that she desired and needed to stay at the company—for financial and emotional reasons—but the line job she had currently did not match her strengths. Using her weakest skills was exhausting her.

Writing out these assessments gave her the focus she needed to take action on her own behalf. She went back to her boss and asked if she could rotate into a staff assignment for a while. He agreed. He valued Ruth and wanted her to stay. He was relieved because he saw that she was becoming less productive as a result of the increasing pressure. Of course the trade-off for Ruth was that she wasn't sure if she would get her job back with her old boss when she decided to return. Was she derailing herself? "I have to take that chance," she said. "My health and state of mind are far more important. What good am I to my family if I can't even enjoy them anymore?"

Two months later I called Ruth to check in with her. I wanted to see if she felt she had made the right choice. The secretary told me that Ruth was no longer at the company, and there was no forwarding number. I called her home and left a message. A few days later she called me back.

"I left the company for a better offer. I'm a vice president with First Central, a competitor, doing the same job. The money is one-third more and I got a ten-thousand-dollar signing bonus."

Four months later, Ruth called me again.

"I left First Central. Can you help me get a job back in my old company?"

"What happened?"

"I couldn't take the pressure. I didn't realize how burnt out I was. The steep learning curve, the new culture, and the pressure were worse than the company I left. I was seduced away. I should have stayed and taken the staff job. I want it back, if they will have me."

The moral of the story: Don't try to take a shortcut to a happy ending. Don't be seduced back into your comfort zone. As Ruth found, it is easy to be seduced if you underestimate your vulnerability to the fear of the unknown, a need to feel financially secure, or the flattery of a good offer.

The exercises and assessment tools in this book are not quick-fix quizzes like those you will find in magazines and newspapers. When you take the time to complete them fully and honestly, they are in-depth barometers of what is going on within you. Once you have determined that it is time for a change, write out your plan and stick to it. Listen to what you say about yourself, take yourself seriously, and *follow your advice.*

FINDING YOUR SONG

Josie, Doug, and Ruth each had a vague sense of what was wrong in their lives and careers, but until they assessed the skills and settings that made them happiest, they were stymied with unclear feelings of stress, frustration, and unfulfillment.

Every person's situation is different, and what brings one person into balance may not satisfy another. Ultimately, you are the only one who knows what you want. To find happiness, you must live by your own standards, following your own agenda—not someone else's. What looks like success to one person may look like failure to someone else. It all comes down to being true to yourself.

This is what your crisis-proof career plan allows you to do: create your own agenda. Short- or long-term, innovative or traditional, if your plan is based on self-knowledge, it will be right for you. Some plans require a huge stretch and much courage; others, such as Doug's, only small commitments. Whatever it is, do it and do it now!

"A bird does not sing because it has an answer," wrote Joan Anglund, "it sings because it has a song." Your crisis-proof career is your song.

## CHAPTER 7

A DAILY REGIMEN FOR SUCCESS
IMPLEMENTING THE PLAN

*I*t is one thing to sit comfortably in your armchair and dream about possibilities, and another to test your dreams in the cold light of reality. In the last chapter you described your crisis-proof career and outlined a strategy to achieve it. Now is the time to act on that strategy. This chapter will give you state-of-the-art tips about how to go out into the marketplace and implement that plan on a day-by-day basis.

This daily regimen provides you with three essentials during your career search: structure, feedback, and support. You need to *structure* your time so that you can pace your efforts, plan logically, and follow through. Without structure, you may squander opportunities and resources, never get organized, or never feel in control. The daily regime gives you daily and weekly action plans and outlines proven methods to make the contacts you need to lead you to the next stage.

Feedback is important because you need to know how you are doing—what's working and what needs to be improved. Included in the daily regime are techniques to help you get feedback from yourself, from your friends and family, and from potential employers.

Support, too, is vital, both from others and from yourself. You need to surround yourself with people who believe in you, who can look past this vulnerable transition and remind you of who you can be. More important is your ability to provide your own support to meet your needs for appreciation and recognition. In giving you these essentials, the daily regimen keeps you moving toward your crisis-proof career.

GETTING STARTED

"I have a new philosophy," said Helen, a former vice president of operations in a securities brokerage. "I'm only going to dread one day at a time."

When Helen was given a year's severance, friends told her she had it made; she could take her job search at an unpressured pace and find something really worthwhile. Helen had lots of entrepreneurial ideas, but as the days and weeks passed, she couldn't seem to get organized. Instead, she spent most of her time between the health club and the tennis club.

Six months later, time was running out. She called me in a panic and we got busy on her crisis-proof career plan. As the answers fell into place, Helen grew more confident. The day she left with her completed plan in her hand, she was smiling.

A month later, I checked in with Helen to see how things were going.

"Terribly! I don't know what it is. I can't seem to keep at it. It's so hard to get motivated when you don't have a job."

"But you do have a job," I said. "A very important one—implementing your career plan."

"What do you mean?"

"Look at it this way. You told me you were ready for something new, something really challenging that would enhance your professional development. You wanted autonomy, the chance to be creative, expand your horizons, and meet interesting people in your field. A career search has every one of these ingredients."

"I guess you're right," Helen said, laughing. "Do you think I'm qualified for the position?" She was beginning to get the idea.

"No one better. Think of the skills you used in your last position: resourcefulness, good organization, and problem-solving skills. You had to pace yourself, keep an eye to the bottom line, and conduct periodic performance reviews to make sure things were on track. You handled details and met deadlines. You maintained a clear image of the big picture to help you steer through the obstacles. Your career search requires these same skills."

"All right, but what, specifically, are my responsibilities?"

"How about this for a job description?

"Position: president of Helen Hill & Company. Sales executive, with eye to bottom line. Chief responsibilities include development and implementation of sales and targeted marketing strategies, including creation and distribution of relevant materials (resumés, cover letters, and contact sheets). Responsible for creating and carrying out daily and weekly action plans, with objectives; design and completion of progress reviews; progress overview in daily appreciation log; develop and maintain professional network of one hundred and twenty-five or more names; attend seminars, conferences, workshops, and social functions on behalf of the organization. Resulting in closing one good sale."

"Sounds great! I'll take it!" she said.

When I checked back with Helen sometime later, she was still upbeat and on target. This way of thinking about her career search had given her the reframing she needed to engage herself in an energetic way.

Considering your career search as a full-time position worthy of your best professional effort can make all the difference in your ability to get moving and keep moving. This attitude allows you to maintain your sense of purpose and self-esteem, two essential assets to help you through your transition into a crisis-proof career. You are no longer "unemployed," but actively engaged in your professional development. You will learn many new career skills, make new contacts, and gain valuable information about your field of interest.

Another advantage to this approach is that it more accurately reflects the actual time and effort required to find your next right career position or to start your own business. Many people make the mistake of thinking they can conduct a successful career search sporadically, a few hours at a time, two or three days a week. They may put off getting started or interrupt their search and lose momentum.

What title would you give yourself? What about employment investigator? Senior vice president of marketing, senior recruitment specialist? Vice president of staffing? If you are sales oriented, imagine that you are working for yourself. You only have to make one big sale on a high-quality, top-of-the-line item—you!

FULL-TIME OR PART-TIME CAREER SEARCH?

Barry works for a software company, but he feels he hasn't yet utilized his potential. He wants to implement his crisis-proof career plan to find something that will. Over the years, Barry has survived many layoffs. "I've learned a lot from my friends who have left. Most of them say it is easier to find a job if you already have one."

I hear this old saw frequently. The fact is, there are advantages and disadvantages to both job and jobless career-search strategies. If you are fortunate enough to have a choice whether to stay or leave, you need to decide which of these strategies is right for you, regardless of what others say.

Among the factors to consider are these: your temperament and tolerance for change and uncertainty; the size of your financial nest egg; how much you enjoy working alone; your level of self-motivation; and finally, how you feel about pursuing your career search for four months or more, nonstop.

Part-time

The primary advantage of having a job while looking for another is that you appear to be making the choice to leave, rather than being forced to. The primary disadvantage of being employed is that you may not be able to put enough time into your search over and above the requirements of your current job.

In weighing your decision, ask yourself the following questions to clarify your feelings and thoughts:

Do you feel more confident and secure having a job while you work on your plan?

Do you get depressed and lethargic during times when there is no outside structure in your life?

Do you like the structure and routine your current job affords?

Do you enjoy going beyond your comfort zone and networking with people outside your company?

Do you feel that someone—an ally, a mentor, a supporter—is going to save you, if you just stay a bit longer?

Can you get away for a few hours for lunch outside your building?

Can you come in late and leave early for networking, interviews, and job seminars?

Can you use the phones, copier, and the secretarial pool with no questions asked?

Do you have a good six months before you actually need to leave?

If you can answer most or all of these questions in the affirmative, you may feel more secure staying in your current job and pursuing your career search on a part-time basis, reserving time each day to make calls, network, and go on interviews.

When Barry considered these questions, he decided to keep his job. He used his flexible hours and home computer to maximize the time he could spend on his search. He scheduled lunch each day with his networking referrals.

For many, Barry's is the right solution. Others find the dual pressure of two demanding jobs more than they can handle effectively. The danger is that you may overextend yourself to the point that your performance suffers. Keep in mind that the real networking clock is only running between eight A.M. and six P.M. each day, so that's when you need to do the bulk of your networking. This means if you are in a high-pressure job with deadlines to meet, you probably need to choose between your job and your career search. If you are serious about implementing your crisis-proof career, you may need to leave your job, create a budget and a financial timetable, take a vacation to decompress, and then look while you are clearheaded and not fettered with too much responsibility.

Full-time

Should you resign? If you have that option, ask yourself the following questions:

Do you have enough money to live for six months while you look?

Are all the other areas in your life fairly stable: your marriage, your finances, your debt-to-savings ratio, your relationship with your children, your feelings about yourself?

Are your moods consistent?

Do you feel capable of structuring your day when there is little or no external structure?

Do you like working out of your house alone most of the day?

Do you feel okay knowing that this is a three-to-six-month effort requiring six to eight hours a day?

Do you have supportive friends to help you through this process?

Do you have a network of 125 or more colleagues, friends, and coworkers or have what it takes to build one?

Do you have some good answers as to why you resigned?

Do you feel confident enough to handle the barrage of questions from recruiters, employers, and colleagues?

If you can answer yes to most or all of these questions, it may be that you have sufficient structure in your life to go on your own. In this case, you may want to resign and work full-time on your crisis-proof career.

If you are still uncertain as to which to do, read through this chapter carefully, thinking in realistic terms about which situation will best enable you to carry out the tasks required to implement your Plan A. You may want to list the pros and cons of each on a piece of paper. If you still can't reach a decision, the best bet is to stay with your present job awhile longer and implement your Plan A from there.

STAGES OF THE CAREER SEARCH STRUCTURE

I often tell clients that the career search resembles a jumbo jet. The jet can't go from standing still to an altitude of 37,000 feet in one motion. It has to be properly serviced, warmed up, taxied to the runway, and accelerated gradually. Only then can it become airborne and reach its cruising altitude.

The same is true with finding the right work. The process requires many steps and stages. All too often, we measure ourselves on the basis of whether we obtained our career objective *that day*. Yet by putting aside such limiting expectations, you can actually come to enjoy the process and obtain a more accurate measure of your progress.

In the months ahead, your search will progress through different stages as it moves from uncertainty to certainty. By becoming aware of these different stages and their purpose, you can structure your approach accordingly for best results.

Stage One: Information Gathering

Typically, the first four to six weeks of a career search consist of talking to many people about what they like and dislike about what they do, so that you can get a sense of what appeals to you. Your goal at this point is to stay open to new possibilities and identify all the options that might satisfy your career goal. If you are a fifty-year-old real estate executive, you'll want to develop a networking list of other middle-aged real estate executives and ask them, "What do middle-aged real estate executives do after leaving a large company? What are my options from your perspective?" If you wonder what it is like to go into business for yourself, ask friends if they know someone who is a sole proprietor in your area of interest.

Stage Two: Focus

After six weeks or so, your goals will become clearer and your options will narrow. As a middle-aged real estate executive, you may have identified some investment bankers who need what you have to offer. You will want to investigate two or three of these possibilities in more depth.

At this stage, your search should be based on a coherent marketing strategy, in which you set clear objectives and conduct market research. Among the techniques you will employ in your strategy—networking, answering want ads, and sending resumés to recruiters, etc.—you will find that some techniques are more effective than others. For example, you will almost certainly derive the most benefit from networking, that is, direct contact with people in face-to-face meetings (including information-gathering and interviews) and telephone calls. This is the "hidden job market" where most people find what they want. The following three steps will guide you in conducting your market research.

1. Remember to refer frequently to your Plan A. For example, take the items you listed in the top critical job factors in chapter 6 and choose your ideal job and setting. Then consult *Dun & Bradstreet* or *Standard & Poor's* (at your library in the business section) or your local chamber of commerce for a list of companies. Make a note of those within your commuting parameters.

2. Make a list of the firms within your area that have some interest for you—twenty-five to fifty will do. Now type this list on a piece of paper or onto your computer.

3. Take this list with you when you meet with friends, coworkers, peers, or colleagues. Ask them, "Look at my target companies. Who do you know in these companies that I might call?" Also ask," Look at this career objective and tell me who you know that I might talk with about this." Ask to use their names. If necessary, revise your resumé so that it reflects specific skills and work experience relevant to this option. If you are starting your own business, you need to identify a product or service, your market, pricing, and a location.

Stage Three: Finding the Openings

You focus on one option and find all the available openings, or all the details you need to cover for your business. You spend most of your day networking on the phone to uncover openings (best option), to get more names of people who might have openings (next-best option), or to get names of people to send your resumé to. Your goal is to set up a meeting with these people, if possible.

If you are starting your own business, you will be identifying your potential customers and calling them. Your goal here is to meet with them in person.

Most people find what they want in stage three. Others, however, do not find their ideal career situation ready-made in the marketplace. If this is true for you, you may need to create your own job situation or invent a new service or product.

Stage Four: Job Innovating

In this stage, you use your networking to identify an unmet need in your ideal work environment. For example, you may have located a company for which you want to work. You create a job for yourself by contacting the appropriate person, explaining how you can satisfy that unmet need, and making an offer to work for them as a project manager or a consultant. If you are in business for yourself, you may identify the needs of your customers and then create a new service or product to meet that need.

A CRISIS-PROOF RESUMÉ

One of the essential materials you will need to distribute during every phase of your search is your resumé. The key difference that sets a crisis-proof resumé apart from other resumés is that a crisis-proof resumé looks ahead to what you want to do with your career, rather than looking behind to where you've been. How does this work? Another way to look at it is to say that on the Find Your Bliss Grid in chapter 3, the first two questions are about safety and security: "Things that I never want to do again" and "Things people say I do well, but I take for granted." Most people fill their resumés with these security-oriented items, then wonder why they keep getting the same routine jobs. The answer is, you get what you ask for.

Crisis-proof candidates concentrate on the other two questions on the grid: "Things I like to do and wouldn't mind doing again" and "Things I'd like to learn more about if I had the time, money, and other resources." They highlight these skills and activities from their previous experiences and expand them into achievements. These are the areas of personal growth and challenge.

Karen enjoyed business development. So she made sure she listed all her previous experience in this area under "Personal Achievements" on her resumé. On the other hand, she minimized or omitted the parts of her job that made it unsatisfying. Why would she seek another chance to do what she disliked or didn't find particularly challenging?

A well-articulated summary of your accomplishments will tell potential employers the direction in which you wish to move, not just where you've been. To write your accomplishment statement, look through all your previous statements and pull out three major skill areas you prize and three characteristics that demonstrate how you take advantage of those skill areas.

Karen wrote "sales management, cash management, business

development, planning, and production management. A creative, innovative manager with strong analytical problem-solving talents."

To write your own accomplishment statement, include the problem or the context in which you worked, what you did to solve the problem, and the quantifiable result.

Ask yourself, *How did I do more with less?* "Launched a campaign to improve sales in product area that resulted in 34 percent increase in revenues utilizing smaller sales force."

How did I find a need and fill it? "Refurbished barn into a wine museum attracting media attention and tourists, resulting in 15 percent increase in sales for company."

How did I find a new twist to an old problem? "Converted payroll manual system to computerized system, increasing efficiency by 60 percent."

While there is no consensus on how to write the perfect resumé, one thing is certain: you have just one minute to grab a potential employer's attention. To do this, your resumé must be concise and well-written; it must be strong enough to entice the reader to pick up the phone and call you for an interview, whether or not he or she has an opening. In essence, a resumé is a marketing brochure and you are the product.

Moira, a senior software manager with a high-tech firm listed "Prom Queen, Branford High School, 1961" under personal accomplishments. She told me her husband thought she should include it. I asked her, "How would that get you a better job now?"

Put yourself in the mind of the reader. If he or she had your ideal career position to offer you, what would he or she be looking for in a candidate to fill it? What qualifications do you have that match a position of this level and this description? How can you best communicate them?

For more information on resumé basics and examples of both a functional and chronological resumé, refer to Appendix A at the end of this chapter.

WEEKLY STRUCTURE

Now that you have an overall view of where you are and have a solid resumé on hand, it's time to get to work. A job search requires weekly objectives and action plans, which you can then break down into smaller and more concrete units of activity. I suggest that you put together a weekly action plan every Sunday night that will specify how you plan to spend your time for the rest of the week. At the end of each day, update your plan for the next. This way you don't have to start out with a blank calendar. Your agenda for the day will be right before you: the names of people you will call, the follow-up meetings you need to schedule, and the letters you need to send. Make your plans realistic, yet challenging. Remember that implementing your career plan is a full-time job, but don't overdo it. Now more than ever, you need balance in your life: work *and* play. Here is a sample Action Plan.

Action Plan for the Week of _____
My objectives for this week are (list as many as necessary):
My objectives for today are:
Activities to accomplish today are:
    8 A.M.
    9
    10
    11
    12 noon
    1 P.M.
    2
    3
    4
    5
    6
    7

Here is how Helen filled out the sheet. Notice that she was working in the third phase of her career search, uncovering the openings.

Helen's Daily Action Plan for the Week of August 22

My objectives for this week are:
    1. Send out 25 marketing letters.
    2. Answer all appropriate ads from the Sunday paper.

3. Send resumé to 25 search firms.

4. Make 30 calls a day and make sure I get 10 completed calls (i.e., reach the influential person or decision maker).

5. Line up 5 networking meetings and uncover 5 job openings. Then reward myself by going on a hike.

My objectives for today are:

1. Make 30 calls and try to get 10 completed calls.

2. Look through the Sunday paper for appropriate ads.

Activities to accomplish today:

8 A.M. Calls until noon

12 noon Lunch with Ralph M. (vice president of Comtec)

2 P.M. More calling until 6

6 P.M. Look through papers, update daily action plan for tomorrow

Performance Incentives

Keep a list of activities you enjoy to reward yourself with when you complete your daily or weekly objectives. If you need suggestions, go back to the Find Your Bliss Grid and look at your answers under "Things I like to do and wouldn't mind doing again." Choose one of the items you can do in the allotted time. Take a nap, a hot bath, ride your bike, garden, make a cup of tea and sit outside and read for half an hour. You deserve it. You've accomplished what you set out to do today.

FEEDBACK AND APPRECIATION

When you plant seeds in your garden, you don't stand next to them and stamp your feet because they aren't growing fast enough. You congratulate yourself for preparing the soil, making the beds, planting the seeds, and watering them each day. You don't feel less a gardener in the planting stage than when you harvest the vegetables or see the flowers. The process is all one, although there are many stages that lead to the successful outcome.

The crisis-proofing process works the same way. You need to appreciate your daily accomplishments. Learn to recognize the small steps toward your goal and see how they contribute to the whole. Keeping a journal can help you see the continuity of your efforts.

Divide an eight-and-a-half-by-eleven-inch spiral notebook into three sections: one for an "appreciation log," one section for a journal of your career search, and one for notes from interviews and meetings. Take time to write in each section each night.

When you sit down to write, begin with your appreciation log. On the top of a new page, put the date and write: *What I appreciated about myself today.* These are items that worked for you or feelings you overcame to continue working during the day. Helen wrote: "Today talking on the telephone to a recruiter about losing my job, I handled his questions in a way that surprised even me! I stretched myself a bit today."

Your career search journal is an important way to track your physical and emotional progress, to hear what you have to say to yourself. Record doubts, ideas, impressions, anything interesting that happened that you might want to remember.

Use the final section for your notes from your interviews and meetings; write down observations about how the sessions went or brainstorm about what you could have done differently. Accumulate "tips" to keep in mind for future reference.

Then, one Sunday night when the thought of another week of career searching weighs heavily on your mind, you will find it rewarding to pick up your notebook and read the entries. You'll see what a pro you've become in handling objections from employers, how resilient you've become in tackling hard questions, both in person and over the telephone, and more. It's valuable to see where you've been and how far you've come. This notebook is a way for you to build some inner resources to guide, inform, and comfort yourself.

CAMPAIGN PROGRESS REVIEW

Every four weeks, complete a campaign progress review. This is a very different way to gauge your progress from reading your log. Here, you tally all the phone calls you completed, all the interviews you went on, all the rejections you received, and all the letters and resumés you sent. Then go over your plans and activities; if possible, do this with a friend or your spouse and ask for feedback on your progress. Discuss any roadblocks you have encountered. How are your interviews going? Are you asking the right questions to get the information you need? Are you making the right contacts?

Look for a pattern. Ask yourself, "What should I do more and what should I do less?" Then change your methods accordingly. Here's a worksheet for your campaign progress review.

Campaign Progress Review

	week 1	week 2	week 3	week 4
# marketing letters sent				
# resumés sent				
# phone calls completed				
# networking meetings				
# interview meetings				
# job offers				
# job rejections				
# want ads sent				

Thomas put a lot of time into attending professional luncheons and workshops where he met some good contacts. At the end of four weeks, however, he noticed that the number of openings he had uncovered did not justify the amount of time he spent on these activities. He changed his strategy and spent more time on the telephone talking with people who were better able to get him what he needed at that stage in his search.

NETWORKING: WHY, WHO, HOW, WHEN, AND WHERE

Networking is the lifeblood of a crisis-proof career. As a career seeker, at least 80 percent of your time should be spent networking, that is, talking to people on the phone or in person, and using these contacts to gain the up-to-date information and personal connections you need for a successful career search.

Networking works for you in four ways:

1. It helps you gather the most current information about industry trends, local trends, and individual companies. I call this *action research* because you gain up-to-the-minute information. Research based on books and periodicals, on the other hand, is quickly outdated.

2. It gives you introductions to people, who then become involved in your success. When a position that interests you opens up, your networking will give you a valuable advocate in the company who has a personal relationship with you.

3. It helps you to discover hidden jobs, those jobs that are never even advertised because they are filled by insiders. Competition for these jobs is less than for advertised positions, and your credibility is higher because you know the person who told you about the job.

4. It gives you interviewing skills, so when the real interview comes along, you've gained valuable experience in telling your story and talking about your accomplishments.

The alternative to networking is the paper campaign. This approach is longer, more expensive, and less effective, as Jake found out. A likable, attractive thirty-two-year-old marketing manager, Jake nevertheless spent two years finding a job because he waged a paper campaign rather than a person-to-person campaign. He sent out letter after letter, resumé after resumé. Frequently, by the time Jake found out about a position, it was already filled. A paper campaign lacks the essential quality of a personal connection that is possible over the telephone or in person. With networking, you can develop rapport, engage people in a dialogue, ask your questions and answer theirs, then follow up with new questions. You become more memorable to the people you contact, and they can see more readily what you might need that they can offer.

Building Your Network

Even if you have not kept a black book or contact file in the past, you probably have the potential for a first-class professional network. Most people have an extensive list of people they know both personally and professionally, and each of those contacts has his own long list. If you get the names of several referrals from each person you know, you widen your circle of contacts exponentially.

Begin by listing everyone you can think of. Don't worry at this point about whether or not they are a "good" contact. There will be plenty of time to cull the list later on.

Take inventory of all your personal contacts. If you can mentally picture their faces, they are personal contacts. The fact that you remember their faces and something about them is the first step in building rapport and trust in any telephone call.

When thinking about your personal contacts, it may help to do this simple exercise. In the middle of a piece of paper, draw a one-inch circle. Label it with your name. Then draw other circles close to yours. These circles represent your closest satellites—your friends, relatives, in-laws, neighbors, church friends, coworkers past and present, college pals, and former bosses. In many respects, these contacts are your biggest asset. They take or return your calls. They are people who know and like you, with whom you have proven credibility. They will be more energetic in their efforts to help you any way they can. You can speak to them confidentially.

Be sure you call on these closest contacts first, before you call anyone else. Don't worry that your personal contacts are not at the decision-making level. They can give you some referrals and put in a good word or two for you.

Next, inventory your professional contacts, those who know you in your professional role. It may be someone traveling in the seat next to you on a plane with whom you struck up a conversation, or someone you met once at a conference. In general, you will find that these people are pleased to help if they can. A professional contact is not necessarily a person who has a job for you, but a person who can lead you to other people at appropriate levels of the executive and professional world.

When you can't think of any more names to put down, try these sources:

Your Christmas-card lists from several years back.

Your checkbook: doctor, dentist, travel agent, stockbroker, optician, therapist, tradesman, drugstore owner.

Your college newsletter or directory of alums from undergraduate or graduate school.

Your files for seminars and conferences, and professional directories of classes you went to in the last five years. Speakers you've met at meetings, other members of your professional societies, members of your church.

Old address books and social acquaintances: golf, swim, tennis, social club members.

Your children's school PTA directories: teachers, children's friends' parents.

Your appointment books for the last seven years.

When you once again come to a standstill, here is another memory jogger. Consider the following categories and try to think of as many people as you can who might fit in each:

Anchors: people who form the core of your network and are fundamental to getting your job done (e.g., a secretary, an assistant).

Experts: people in your field whom you respect and value as professionals.

Supporters: people in related fields who help you get your job done (a tax accountant, lawyer, house cleaner).

Mentors, formal or informal: people who have helped guide your career, provided opportunities, or taught you the ropes.

Role models: people who inspire you, whose professional behavior stimulates your ideas for the future.

Matchmakers: people who suggest helpful connections, sources of information—they are well connected and know lots of people.

Confronters: people who force you to ask questions, to look at yourself, and look at where you're going in life.

Recommenders: people in your field whom you value and respect.

Once you have as large a list as you can generate, go through and rank each person on a scale of 1 to 5. Do they have decision-making power or do they know what is going on? The highest-ranking people should be those you know best: colleagues, former bosses, peers, former peers, and suppliers and clients with whom you have had good and long-term relationships. Also rank as 1 all who know people, who are matchmakers, catalytic, and influential. Reserve a 5 for those you know by reputation only or haven't known very long.

Using this list, you never have to cold call or talk to a stranger again. Following the network approach outlined here, you will always have a name to open the next door.

How to Structure Your Network

In this job market, people are constantly changing jobs and moving up, out, and around. The person you met as a vice president in marketing last year may be COO of a small medical products company next year. It pays to keep in touch.

How you go about organizing your files is a matter of personal preference. Some people like a binder, others a card file. Some prefer a chronological listing, others alphabetical. Here are some suggestions in both formats.

Chronological. In this system you record when you contacted a person on your list so that you can know when to follow-up or check in again. Some clients list all their contacts on eight-and-a-half-by-eleven notebook paper and keep their daily calls in a three-ring binder format (see example below). Some clients use their computer to list all this information and sort it according to date of most recent calls.

Your chronological networking worksheets should look something like this:

NAME/PHONE NO./ADDRESS/RELATIONSHIP/DATE OF CONTACT/STATUS/
FOLLOW-UP

1.
2.
3.
4.

Alphabetical. An alternative format is to build a three-by-five (or four-by-six) card file that includes all the people you have met and talked to. On the left, list the contact's name, title, address, and telephone number. On the right, list the referral source and some personal information about the contact you can use to build rapport and to start off the conversation. Note when to check back with the person again. You can also collect business cards from people you have met and staple these cards to your three-by-five cards. File them alphabetically and keep them handy in an accessible place. Write your reactions and notes on the back of each card to remind you of opportunities, your reactions at the time of introduction, interesting points of conversation, and interests shared. The advantage of this option is that they are compact enough to carry around and you can sort them. You can move the ones you must call to the top of the card pack.

Sample of Networking Connection on a 3 × 5 Card

Name	Who referred me to this person
Title	Relevant facts
Address	Dates called
City/State	Follow-up
Zip Code	
Phone number	

Whatever way you want to organize yourself is fine. But do organize! Without a system, you are courting disaster, as Glenn found out. He had bundled scraps of paper and scribbled notes taped in a spiral notebook. He was never quite sure that he was on top of things. As it happened, he wasn't. He missed his chance to follow up on a position that went to someone else.

Don't forget to stay in touch with your contacts. Remember to send thank-you letters to all those you spoke with and give them appreciative feedback. Then follow up with additional contacts such as phone calls, notes, news clippings on topics of mutual interest, or an invitation to lunch. Take the initiative, show interest. I love to send an apropos *New Yorker* cartoon to someone I recently met, just to have them keep me in mind.

Keep track of how many times you call and what is said, so next time you can start up where you left off. Refresh the person's memory about the last conversation you had and what you discussed.

Once you have developed a working network, be sure to be on the lookout for new people. Make it a goal to add ten new people to your network every month. Join professional organizations, attend seminars, and make the effort to introduce yourself to new people.

You can keep adding and updating your list for the remainder of your career and will find innumerable uses for it. Don't be like Brenda. On the Saturday night before she started work at her new job, she made a big fire in her fireplace to celebrate. She gleefully got all her boxes of contacts and burned them. "I won't be needing these anymore!" she exclaimed. A year later she was laid off again and she had to start from scratch. People do silly things!

After you find your next position, don't withdraw. Help others. Be a resource by sharing contacts. If someone is unemployed now, he or she will be employed soon enough.

Getting Started: When to Contact

Once you have a lengthy list, *when* do you contact *whom*? If you have been laid off or have left work, I suggest that you contact only the most supportive people during the first several weeks. Choose friends who can be enthusiastic advocates of your search and emotionally available. They will send you to their friends to talk about jobs. With these people, you can test your strategies and your answers to their questions. You'll need some practice to sharpen up your interviewing style, and you can practice on them with nothing to lose. During the first six weeks you don't need to focus—just get the lay of the land.

Once you feel more confident, or if you are currently employed, you can go on to the next phase, which is to contact people who have influence and power. These are people who have or know of jobs through their networks of business friends. But don't underestimate all kinds of contacts along the way—one of my clients landed a job she heard about while talking to a checker at her local supermarket.

Networking Techniques: Conquering Fear

Many, many people experience telephone fear when they begin networking.

"Why would they want to talk to me?"

"I feel uncomfortable asking for help."

"I hate to talk to strangers."

As a career seeker, it is easy to feel this way. But now put yourself in the other person's shoes. What if someone contacted you for some information you had at your fingertips? Or called to talk on a subject of professional interest to you? Most people enjoy being helpful and making a new contact.

Approach people with the attitude that they can and want to help. As you become more adept at networking and sharing information, you will see that you, too, have something to offer in every telephone conversation.

My clients have found the following suggestions helpful in their efforts to overcome their fear and enjoy networking—in spite of themselves!

How to Make Strangers Fast Friends

1. Start your day by calling supportive personal contacts first. This gives you ballast and confidence to work up the momentum to call referrals.

2. As you talk on the telephone, get your energy going by standing up, walking, or pacing. Put a smile on your face.

3. Close your eyes and concentrate on your voice and what it conveys. Send warmth. Create a picture in your mind of the person on the other end of the telephone.

4. Picture your voice flowing through the wire and making friends with that other voice.

5. Write a telephone script, one that is short but asks a lot of open-ended questions (see the suggestions below).

6. Remember each call has an objective. Jot that objective down on a piece of paper before you call and keep it in front of you while you talk.

7. Find something that has value for you and for the other person. Answer the question "Why should he/she talk to me?" before you pick up the phone.

Telephone Script

Perhaps the most helpful device to overcome telephone fear is to develop telephone scripts for all occasions: one script for people you don't know well, one for referrals, and one for getting reacquainted with a former friend or coworker. With a script to jump-start you, you feel prepared. You can use it if you need to or disregard it once the conversation begins to flow. Keep it near the phone so it's handy in case the other party returns your call unexpectedly.

Take the following ideas and brainstorm with a friend to create telephone scripts to fit your needs.

1. Build rapport and credibility. The first step is to find a common interest with the other person. The best way to do this is to remember to get more than just the name and phone number when given a reference. Ask for some personal details about this person: a professional organization, how they know one another, where he or she lives, and any pertinent details about his or her lifestyle. This information enables you to start your conversation with something that shows you are interested in the person, not what he or she has to give you.

For example, you might say, "Jerry suggested that I call. He told me you also belong to the Association of Marketing Managers. I do, too. How often do you go?"

2. Create a dialogue. Don't monopolize the conversation. As in the above example, end your statements with questions—not yes-or-no questions, but open-ended questions that allow the other person to talk. This gives you yet more information on which to build rapport.

3. Create some value for the referral. The secret of networking is to remember that it is a time to give as well as take. You need to develop rapport with your contacts and offer them something of value. Speak on a specific topic of interest to them, especially if it is something in your field. As you pursue your career search, you are steadily gaining more and more knowledge—in fact, you are turning into an expert with access to the latest information. Think what you can offer in the way of information or networking that would cause the person to want to talk or meet with you.

Jim was keenly interested in starting his own business as a software manufacturer and used his knowledge and interest in one aspect of the field to connect with his referrals. He would ask peers if they knew of anyone he could talk with about his ideas.

Jim said, "I am developing a software product to go with Microsoft Windows. In fact, I am delivering a speech on it at a conference next month. Joe told me that you were the guy to talk to about this. Can I meet with you? Anything I use at the conference, of course, I'll credit to you. When can we talk?"

Jim appealed to the referral's desire for recognition. He got an appointment to meet with the man. Notice that Jim didn't ask for a job; he asked for information. He tried to engage his contact's curiosity in an area of mutual interest and the project he was developing.

Here's another example:

Jim: "Merle, our mutual friend, suggested that I speak with you about my idea."

Bob: "How is Merle doing?"

Jim: "Oh, Merle is getting promoted. He sends his regards. How long have you known him?"

Bob: "Merle and I go way back. We went to Whitman together. How do you know him?"

Jim: "Merle and I went to Harvard Business School. That's when he got interested in computer applications. How familiar are you with that area?"

Sometimes, particularly in the earlier phase of your career search, you won't have an idea you can use like this. Think of another topic of mutual interest. If you have heard or read an interesting fact or opinion, ask if the other person also heard or read this. If not, tell about it in a few short sentences. Ask what they think about it.

4. Calibrate the types of information you need. Set up clear expectations for the networking call or meeting. Know the job you want or know the skills you want to use. It is not the contact's responsibility to uncover what you want. Be brief. For example: "I want a job as manager of a marketing department" or "I want to use my marketing, planning, and organizing skills. Where in your company is that compatible?" "From your experience, do you feel my abilities fit? With whom should I be talking?"

Talk briefly about your accomplishments and end with a question:

"Last year I brought in six hundred thousand dollars' worth of business for Kanyer in marketing and delivery. Are these the kind of accomplishments that are of interest to you?"

Some clients say, "Any way you slice it, I'm still asking for a job. I don't like to put myself in a needy situation."

I say, "No, you are looking for information that can uncover a job." There is a big difference.

In the telephone script you can ask:

"These are my skills [name three] and this is my career objective [name it]. Where would they be compatible in your company?"

"If you were me, with whom would you be talking within your firm?"

If you were me, with whom would you be talking within your network?

"Do you know of any openings in your firm?"

"Do you know of any opportunities in your field?"

You must think of these contacts as people within your ongoing professional network, not onetime calls. When you have a particularly good conversation with someone, end the conversation in such a way as to allow you to follow up. For example, "I will call you in a month to let you know my progress."

"Thank you for your suggestions. May I follow up with you in several months after I see how they turn out?"

Or you might close with: "In the meantime, I'd like to send you my resumé for you to look over."

"Can I get back to you in several weeks? I'd just like to check in because things change very rapidly nowadays."

It is a courtesy to report back when contacts have given you a good referral, to thank them and acknowledge their help. This, too, gives you another opportunity to talk to them and get more ideas. Stay informal, genuine, upbeat, and professional.

I will never forget the man who kept calling me when I was in a hiring position. He wasn't qualified for the opening, but he was so upbeat and professional that I didn't mind when he called. In fact I enjoyed it because he always had a tidbit of information to give me. He'd say, "I saw an article in the *New York Times* about outplacement the other day, did you see it?" If I hadn't, he would send it to me. I finally said, "I enjoy talking to you, and I genuinely want to help you, what can I do?"

Networking Performance Checklist

As you continue your calls, it is important to gain some idea of how you are doing. You can gain some important feedback by considering these statements after each call:

1. I had a clear objective for the call.
2. I made notes or wrote a script in preparation for the call.
3. I asked for and used the secretary's or assistant's name.
4. I used his or her name in thanking him or her.
5. I introduced myself and mentioned the purpose of my call.
6. I used referral sources to gain the person's interest.
7. I got to the point promptly.
8. I stated the objective of the call.
9. I presented my job change positively.
10. I captured the contact's interest by mentioning something he/she was curious about early on in the conversation.
11. I avoided asking for a job.
12. I avoided being interviewed extensively by telephone.
13. I avoided mailing my resumé if I could set up a meeting.
14. I suggested times and dates for an appointment.
15. I creatively negotiated any roadblocks to an appointment.
16. I got the desired appointment or I got an alternative name to call.
17. I clarified address, floor, room, etc.
18. I offered a phone number where I could be reached in case of a change in plans.
19. I made notes of the conversation and the appointment immediately afterward.

Other Networking Opportunities

It is important to incorporate social functions into your career search strategy so that you can meet new people and get the word out that you are looking. Attend conferences, seminars, and social events sponsored by professional organizations. With some planning, you can use these occasions to uncover a job.

Once again, preparation is important. When you arrive, don't just jump in; stand aside. Size up who is with whom, who looks interesting.

Your goal should be to meet one or two new people that work for a company of interest to you. That means talking to several people, perhaps, until you hit the right ones. "Is there anyone here from Apple Computer?" you might ask the host or a fellow participant.

Relax if you can, socialize, and have a good time. Be curious about people. Find out who they are, what they do, their lifestyle and interests.

Sell yourself as a professional at these gatherings, someone with marketplace skills, not an unemployed person. Again, use information you've gained in your search that you are truly interested in talking to people about, just as Jim talked about his pet project. This is a way of developing genuine relationships.

GETTING THE MOST FROM YOUR INTERVIEWING

The goal of your resumé and telephone conversations is to obtain an interview with a prospective employer (or, if you are starting a business, a meeting with potential customers). While the primary purpose of interviewing is to land a job or gain a customer, it can be much more than that. Interviewing can afford you an opportunity to gain valuable feedback and networking information that can make a difference in future interviews.

All interviewers look for three things: competence, chemistry, and communication skills. Competence is the ability to show mastery in your field. Most interviewers gain a sense of your competence through your resumé, talking informally with colleagues who recommend you, and your ability to speak the technical language during the interview. Competence in itself, however, is not enough. Ninety percent of the time, people are hired and fired on the basis of chemistry and communication. You can be the smartest and most technically competent person in the world, but if you cannot demonstrate good interpersonal skills—what I call chemistry—and communicate clearly, you will not get the job. By developing your networking and interviewing skills you can acquire these marketable qualities.

Begin the interview by developing rapport. Small talk, shared experiences, mutual interests, your gratitude at the interviewer's setting aside the time, complimenting his or her good taste in office furniture—all these serve to build rapport and trust.

Next, introduce the agenda and state the purpose of the meeting. Outline the time frame and the content of what you want to uncover. It is important to state these in clear and concise terms. Don't say you came in to "shoot the breeze" or "I was hoping you could tell me what's new in the industry." These are too vague. Also, phrases such as "Jim said I should pick your brain" minimize the referral's expertise and the value of the time they are giving up to meet with you.

You may be asked to tell the interviewer about yourself. Just give the highlights: where you were born and raised, where you went to school, your previous jobs, and why you are looking today. He or she doesn't expect you to drone on for ten minutes nonstop; the interviewer can always follow up with more questions if appropriate. Remember, this is a selling situation, not true confessions.

Work to develop the relationship by creating a dialogue, one that conveys your genuine curiosity and interest in the person and the firm, rather than evaluation or judgment. For 80 percent of the interview you should be listening and asking questions to learn what it is the employer or client wants. What type of person or service is he/she looking for? What skills would a successful candidate possess or a successful product possess? Once you gain a sense of what he/she is looking for, try to fit your accomplishments to those needs. If he/she is looking for a credit person, discuss your accomplishments in solving credit problems.

To create a dialogue, answer the interviewer's question, then ask a question of your own. In doing so, you demonstrate your ability to build relationships and communicate, both of which demonstrate your interpersonal competence. At the same time you will be more likely to get the information you need.

Don't forget to gain feedback from the interviewer you can use to prepare for the next interview. At the end of the interview, you can ask," I've spent the last hour with you and told you a lot about my accomplishments. I am curious about your level of interest at this point." If the interviewer looks confused, help him/her by suggesting, "Is it low, moderate, or high?" If the interviewer says "high," then you say, "What appealed to you about what I said? What had value for you?" If the answer is "low" or "moderate," ask, "What are the factors that keep your rating at moderate?" The interviewer, if honest, will tell you some of his/her concerns that you may otherwise not have known. At this point, it is up to you to address those concerns.

For example, the interviewer might say, "I am concerned that you are overqualified." You might respond, "What did I say that made you think that?"

This gives the interviewer an opportunity to share his/her thinking, and the exchange may give you the chance to change his/her mind. You might say, "Yes, I can understand how you might think that, but don't you need someone who already knows the ropes, so it won't take months and money to train him?"

After the interview, always send a handwritten thank-you note. Interviewers have told me that a thank-you letter was at times all that broke the tie between two accomplished candidates.

NOURISHING THE SPIRIT

Crisis-proofing your career is one of the hardest things you'll ever do, and you need all the support you can get. At the same time, it may be difficult to obtain the type of feedback you need from others. This is a good time to learn that the most valuable feedback comes from within. In the end, your evaluation of yourself is the only one that really matters.

Be kind to yourself. Recognize that this is a vulnerable time when you may feel stretched to the limit by your daily efforts. Do what you can to be nourishing, even protective, of yourself. Put a moratorium on activities that frighten you, such as watching the six-o'clock news, meeting with coworkers who are too probing, going to unemployment groups where everyone gets into a "pity party," unsolved mysteries, or even reading the headlines. When the unemployment figures appear, remind yourself that you don't have to find jobs for 8.6 million unemployed people, just one crisis-proof career for yourself.

Keep up your morale by becoming involved in a class or an

organization where you can learn something interesting that is tangential to your career. Ralph chose a dream group. Sally took a computer course. The value of these outside interests is to give you new experiences and take your mind off your search. In addition, you'll find yourself among diverse people who are not caught up in the job hunt. In fact, they may even be in a position to assist you. Don't forget to add them to your network.

SUPPORT FROM WITHIN: AFFIRMATIONS, VISUALIZATIONS, GROUNDING, AND RITUALS

Your daily attitude is one of the most important factors in your career search. You must believe in yourself if you are going to sell yourself to others. If you start out each morning with a negative attitude, you will sabotage yourself before you have even begun.

At the beginning of the day, you can prepare your frame of mind and get yourself in the mood to talk and meet with people. Just as an actor or actress prepares for the performance or an athlete warms up before the big game, you can discover and practice rituals and routines to replenish your self-esteem and give yourself the emotional nourishment you need.

There are many different techniques people use to achieve a positive frame of mind. Choose the one(s) right for you.

Affirmations

Affirmations can be a powerful asset in positive thinking when they are used to address the self-defeating thoughts that sabotage our efforts. In chapter 4, you were asked to keep a journal of your self-defeating thoughts. Return to those entries and see which of those you may have been encountering in recent days or weeks. Then, construct an affirmation to attack each self-defeating thought. Create affirmations that will spur you on your career search by encouraging you to imagine the best outcome for the day. Here are some guidelines:

1. Always put affirmations in the present tense, rather than in the future.

2. Always phrase affirmations in the most positive way. Avoid *don't, never, or no.* This insures that you can create the best image in your mind.

3. Always start out an affirmation with *I* and your name. "I [your name] now have a wonderful new job."

4. Keep your affirmations short and to the point. It is best if they express a strongly felt desire. Longer ones lose their impact and become intellectual. Say "I [your name] have the career I want now." Not "I hope to try to find something in the near future that suits me, and make lots of money."

Here are some affirmations that have helped my clients get past their self-defeating thoughts each morning before they start their day:

1. I [your name] am free from anger and resentment of the past, and I am finding my right place of work now.

2. I [your name] am open to receive the right work with the right salary in the right location now.

3. I [your name] am now attracting the best work situation into my life.

Put these affirmations on three-by-five cards and keep them in front of the telephone. Read them over at least three times during the day. Act as if these affirmations have already happened. Cary Grant said that back in the early 1930s, when he was a nobody in Hollywood, he decided to counteract his insecurity by acting as if he were a big star. One day years later, he realized that he was no longer acting. He *was* a big star!

Visualization

It is easy to feel powerless during a transition, when improvements happen slowly and our dreams seem to depend on factors beyond our control. In this frame of mind, we overlook the fact that there are many aspects of our situation we *can* control. It is helpful to keep these in mind.

You are in control of your attitude. When you choose to think positively, you can actually bring about more positive outcomes.

You are in control of whom you call and whom you talk to.

You are in control of defining your market, creating your strategy, and implementing your plan.

You are in control of how you talk about or market your skills and accomplishments.

You are in control of the activities with which you fill your day.

Write your career plan on a three-by-five card. Then on another card, write the goal as an affirmation. For example, "I [your name] am now enjoying meaningful work as a [you fill in the blank]. It provides me with financial and emotional fulfillment." Keep these cards in front of you where you make your calls.

Select one of the visualizations in chapter 5 and follow it through your ideal day. When you have finished this, you are ready to start the active part of the day.

Grounding

Grounding is a good way to stay emotionally balanced during this kaleidoscopic time. Those who use it say it helps them feel centered throughout the day, regardless of what is going on around them, so that they can remain calm on the phone and during interviews. It helps them to communicate confidence.

George Leonard, an aikido master and author of the book *Mastery*, suggests you picture your body with steel rods going down from your legs to the center of the earth, and seeing steel threads going from the top of your head to hooks in the sky. In your belly, imagine a ball of light. With these images of strength, you maintain a steady mind and spirit throughout the day.

Rituals

A ritual is an activity you engage in every day that allows you time to be alone with yourself to straighten and gather your thoughts. Charles gets up at six A.M. and jogs two miles, repeating his affirmations. Karen visualizes what the best outcome of the day might be. Sue reads a chapter from an inspirational book before she even gets out of bed. (At the end of this chapter is a short list of inspirational readings that my clients have found useful in their crisis-proofing.) Really, the possibilities are endless. The goal is to find the ritual that allows you the quiet and solitude you need.

A LITTLE HELP FROM MY FRIENDS

Crisis-proofing need not be a solitary process. Often, when the job search bogs down, friends and family can give you the feedback you need to keep going. An exciting way to brainstorm is to throw a career planning party for yourself. Invite friends you know from many different situations but who don't know each other—your lawyer, your sister's friend, your best friend, your doctor, your accountant, your hairstylist, your child who is home from college, your old college buddy, your husband, your mother-in-law. Invite a minimum of five and a maximum of ten. Inviting fewer people allows more time for everyone to get to know each other and have more time to talk in depth about you and each other. Be sure to invite people who enjoy giving praise and appreciation. Beforehand, choose one of your guests to act as facilitator in the discussion. That way, you'll be able to sit back, take notes, and listen.

Serve the food and drinks at the outset of the party to encourage people to mingle and talk. Don't serve alcoholic beverages, which can make people act different from usual. After a time, clear the area and have people seat themselves. Go around the room and tell the group how each person came into your life, why you asked them here, and ask each to introduce him or herself. Then have the facilitator ask each friend for some feedback about what they see about you that they appreciate. What skills do you have that they admire, that you perhaps take for granted? On the basis of what they know about you, have them brainstorm about where they see you working, what would be the ideal day for you, the ideal career for you, etc.

Liz wanted to go into retail sales, but she couldn't find an idea that excited her. Previously, she had worked for a big retailer in their mail order department, designing and producing their seasonal catalogs.

She invited some of her friends to her career planning party. She told them the purpose of the party and to come with their ideas. She began by introducing people, telling why they were invited: Marti was there because she knew Liz from her former job and inspired Liz to work hard. Char had been a coworker who frequently offered objective criticism. Rick was invited because he was a risk-taker, and Diane was strong willed. Dee was an artist and a creative thinker. All these traits were those that Liz admired in her friends.

At Liz's request, Marti threw out the question: "What are some of the things Liz could do, things she might not have thought of? What are some things that could capture her imagination?" Char was the first to ask: "What's not being handled in the fields you want to work in?" While others were brainstorming, Liz's sister Sondra was videotaping the session for Liz to view later.

"I always think of you as an outdoors person," said Rick. "I always enjoy hearing about your backpacking trips."

"What about becoming a wilderness tour guide?" said another friend.

"I always think of how you enjoy your work in creating catalogs, meeting the deadlines, and the pride you take in the finished product," said Char. "You have a real eye for detail."

Liz sat back and listened, not saying anything. She knew the goal was to generate some creative thinking, not to get definitive answers.

In the end, Liz chose to go into a mail order catalog business selling backpacking supplies. It had never occurred to her that she could turn her hobby into her profession. Her friends were able to share a perspective about her that she was too close to see.

Wally was another client who decided he needed some help in the decision-making of his midlife career. So he, too, threw a party.

"Dear Friends," read the notice Wally sent out to ten friends and professional associates, "As you're aware, there has been a great deal of change in my work environment in the last few years: new senior officers, a market-driven company, VRI, competition, OIIs, OIRs, BUD, a new logo, Business Units, profit centers, a different car for the carpool, and on and on. While not every one of these changes has affected me personally, the sum of these changes has increased the level of stress, anxiety, and uncertainty of the future to the point where I have decided to accelerate my midlife crisis to age thirty-nine, rather than waiting until the traditional age of forty.

"Please join me in observing ('celebrating' is too upbeat, 'commiserating' too down) my midlife crisis with a career planning party on Friday, April 22, at 5:00 P.M. at Mickey's Monkey. Come prepared to share the secrets to your success and happiness! We will have the back room for ourselves."

DISCOVERING THE ADVENTURE

"You get the adventure you are ready for," said Joseph Campbell, author and chronicler of myths we live by. I've never seen it more true than in the career search. A crisis-proof career is an adventure that begins with a new view of yourself, your life, and the work you do in it. The more you extend yourself in this process, the more you will grow, and the farther you can reach toward your goals.

Recently, a client said to me, "You know, when I was laid off from the bank five years ago, I was really frightened. I thought I would die, literally die, if I was unemployed. The strategy of making a Plan A and Plan B, and then the day in and day out implementation of networking, the telephone script, and the interview strategies, really worked to keep me going. It was like taking something very frightening and breaking it into smaller and smaller pieces. Like so many baby steps, I would just work with each one and not get overwhelmed by the whole thing. And I did it—I got the job I was after. Then, two years ago, my company decided to leave the area and move to Georgia. They asked me to come, but I didn't want to live in the South, so I decided not to go. I had the courage to leave, knowing full well I would have to do the same job search all over again. But this time, I didn't feel as if I would die. I felt uncomfortable and anxious, maybe; excited, sometimes; die, no. That's when I realized I had crisis-proofed my career. Now I have these tools that I can use again and again. I've never felt stronger and better. I kept saying to myself, 'I only need one job,' And after several months I found an incredible one! I never thought I would ever say that losing your job isn't so bad."

Your adventure doesn't begin the day you first assume your new job or open for business. It begins the moment you take action on your dreams. The best way I know to survive this intensive process of research, networking, and follow-through is to become curious.

Become curious about what you need to know and take the first steps toward your new career. Become curious about the people you talk to, their experiences, their ideas. You can even become curious about yourself and the changes and growth you are experiencing as a result of your career search. Most of all, become curious about your own adventure and where it will ultimately lead you.

APPENDIX A: RESUMÉ BASICS

Be sure to select the appropriate format for your resumé. Do you want to sort your resumé according to function and skills or chronologically? If you want to shift your career slightly, a functional resumé (such as Karen's in the example following) is better. If you are looking for a position based on steady progressive responsibility, a chronological resumé (such as Todd's) is better.

Begin your resumé with your name, address, and phone number. Be sure this telephone is answered professionally and has an answering machine to receive messages when you are not available. It is disconcerting for callers when the phone is answered by a five-year-old or rings endlessly.

Put the name you want to be called on your resumé. Don't put G. James Kirk if you want to be called Jim Kirk.

Clearly state your career objective, either on the resumé or in your cover letter. It is not the employer's job to make sense out of your life.

Put all the critical information in easy-to-locate places, and do not go into great detail. Remember, your resumé is the appetizer to whet the employer's appetite to meet you, not surfeit him or her. You can fill in the particulars during the interview.

List all your past accomplishments. Emphasize titles, numbers, and names. Choose words carefully and delete the unnecessary.

Begin each accomplishment with an action verb. Use *spearheaded, launched,* and *pioneered* rather than overused and lackluster words such as *served, held, managed,* and *implemented.* Employers want results-oriented doers. Take out any *responsible for* or *duties included.* These kill interest.

Tell the employer the breadth, scope, depth, and level of your job by using numbers or percentages of increase. These create credibility.

Numbers show magnitude. Are you a big-league player or a sandlot player? Titles show that someone respected you enough to vest authority in you.

List education on the second page. If you have no entries under education, skip it. Don't drum up seminars and workshops unless they directly relate to your career objectives or skills you can add to the job.

Omit most personal data, including clubs, religious affiliations, or items that might label you and cause sexist, racist, or discriminatory evaluations. However, you might want to include any affiliations that show your authority or your ability to bring in business. This would include country clubs, community memberships, and professional organizations.

Show your resumé to your colleagues to critique for credibility and technical accuracy.

Print only twenty-five copies at a time. You may find it necessary to correct or revise your resumé as you gain feedback or learn more about your search. Don't be like my former client Steve. I visited his home for dinner one night and saw two cartons full of resumés in the hall. When I asked him about it, he laughed and told me he had printed up a thousand copies and then found a typo. So now it's scrap paper for his kids' crayon drawings. His children will be in college by the time it's all gone.

The Cover Letter

Accompany each resumé you send out with an appropriate cover letter. As in the example below, the letter should be brief, upbeat, and conversational. It should serve as a friendly greeting and give you the chance to state your objective in sending your resumé.

Todd E. Hood
250 South Mercedes
Los Angeles, CA 90002
(213) 934-8403

August 17, 1993

Mr. Bob Blatchnow
Zenco Corporation
111 Merit Ave
San Jose, OR 96555

Dear Bob:

I am seeking a position as general manager/CEO of a consumer products company.

I have enclosed my resumé, which highlights my more than twenty years of professional experience and accomplishments in marketing and sales. As you will note, my career has included steady growth throughout and has been characterized by a strong orientation to getting results.

I would appreciate the opportunity to meet with you and discuss my background and opportunities in greater detail. To that end, I will give you a call next week.

Sincerely,

Todd E. Hood

encl.

Chronological Resumé

Todd E. Hood
250 South Mercedes
Los Angeles, CA 90002

(213) 934-8403

CAREER OBJECTIVE: GENERAL MANAGER/CEO

Summary: 20 years experience in consumer products with demonstrated track record in consistently doubling sales and launching a series of profitable new products. Energetic and highly creative manager.

WORK EXPERIENCE

1985 to present   Executive Vice President, Marketing and Sales, Sweet Dreams Mattress Company (A privately held manufacturer of premium hybrid mattresses)

Doubled the size of the company from $27.7 million in sales to $53.6 million in sales while improving profitability from 5% to 8.2%, an increase of 315%.

Launched 2 new product categores and added 5 models to the existing line.

Spearheaded national consumer advertising.

Restructured and revamped the sales force.

Staffed marketing department and set up a customer service department.

Chaired the executive committee and sat on the board of directors.

1983–1985   Vice President, Category Management
                    1984–1985
                    Vice President, New Business
                    1983–1984
                    Brakeco Toys

Increased the preschool toy business from $80 million to $140 million.

Launched a profitable new infant toy line of $30 million in sales.

Built 3 major new product-development areas—children's books, games, and videocassettes—representing $100 million in sales.

1978–1983   **Corporate Vice President, New Products**
                  1980–1983
                  Vice President, Marketing 1978–1980
                  Compulsion Toiletries Company

Doubled the size of the company from $79 million in sales to $161 million while improving profitability. This represents a major turnaround of a 5-year trend of declining sales and profitability.

Launched 5 profitable new products: Obsession Millionaire, High Stick Antiperspirant, Hound, Baby Warm Bath Cloths, and Lady High Stick.

Consolidated the division's efforts on major brands, deleted 36 SKUs, and realigned the way the sales force called on the retail trade.

Doubled the advertising budget to $35 million.

1977   **Senior Vice President of Marketing**
                  Perfect Puff Donuts

Added network television and consumer promotion programs that broadened the business base and increased traffic count. As these programs came on stream the sales increased at the rate of 16% annually.

1972–1977   **Vice President, Growth and Development**
                  Smiles Laboratores, Consumer Products
                  Group

Launched 3 products nationally: Centrix-2, a chewable antacid, One Plus Minerals, a life extension, and Long Years, a multiple vitamin. These were the first profitable major new products the company had launched in 5 years.

1966–1972   **New Ventures Director 1970–1972**
                  New Products Manager 1969–1970
                  Product Manager 1966–1969
                  Gilford Corporation

1965–1966   Product Manager, Grocery Products
                   Division
                   Williams Company

1962–1964   Sale Representative
                   General Food Corporation Pudding
                   Division

EDUCATION

1962   University of Maryland, B.B.A.
                   Marketing
1965   Graduate School of Business, Unversity
                   of Chicago, M.B.A.

Functional Resumé

Karen Rosenwald
350 Circle Avenue
Newark, CA 94910

CAREER OBJECTIVE

An executive-level position in sales management, strategic planning, and business development.

SUMMARY

22 years experience in sales management, cash management, business development, planning, and production management. A creative, innovative manager with strong leadership skills emphasizing teamwork, development of personnel, and results. Strong analytical problem-solving talents.

WORK EXPERIENCE

1979–Present	Pacific Republic Bank, N.A., San Francisco, CA
1984–Present	Retail Banking Group Vice President and District Manager Vice President and Branch Manager
1979–1984	Corporate Banking Group Vice President/Cash Management Consultant
1971–1978	Taylor Trailer Company, Chicago, IL, Cash Manger
1966–1971	Branck-Schwaker Insurance Agency, Chicago, IL, Cash Manager

MAJOR ACCOMPLISHMENTS

Restored performance and image of $600MM core deposit flagship office of Pacific Republic Bank as a result of the Pioneer Valley merger, contributing over $12MM in profit to the company.

Improved aggregate sales performance from below goal to 200% of goal.

Reduced account run off from 24% to 3.6%.

Implemented business development calling program generating over $1.6MM in loans to small businesses, an improvement of 1,000% over previous year.

Initiated telemarketing, time management, and business development training to staff of 45, in addition to bank-packaged programs.

Improved district performance ranking to #2 from #22 of 9-branch district, growing core deposits by 18%; responsible for 100 employees.

Created a positive district team vision in a group of branches historically known for low morale.

Clarified performance plans for 8 branch managers by setting measurable financial and campaign goals, and establishing criteria for performance evaluation.

Trained 75 branch managers in sales and sales management skills.

Implemented training programs for sales, product, and self-improvement for over 100 people.

Recruited and trained 3 nonbanking and 3 banking individuals for branch manager positions, all assigned within 90 days of hire.

Consolidated $20MM branch into $45MM office, retaining 92% of core deposit base of the closing office.

PLANNING

Identified and located $40MM intracompany deposit runoff, created by a merger, explaining variance in retail bank financial plan.

Streamlined flagship branch through staff reduction and relocating operations activities to centralized centers, saving over $146K in salary expense, improving productivity of sales staff, and eliminating customer wait time.

Established customer service and problem resolution standards, reducing the number of monthly customers compalints from 25 to 0.

PRODUCTION MANAGEMENT

Reorganized backshop operations, reducing backlog from 60 days to 24-hour turnaround.

Achieved 5-minute maximum customer wait time on teller line, reducing average wait by 40 minutes.

Consolidated 2 safe-deposit locations with combined capacity of 12,000 safe-deposit boxes.

BUSINESS DEVELOPMENT

Recognized as top cash-management salesperson 3 years consecutively.

Educated financially unsophisticated California middle-market companies, designing and implementing cash-management systems.

Conducted quarterly cash-management seminars for the American Management Association attended by over 200 financial executives of major national coporations. Guest speaker on cash-management topics for professional organizations, including CPAs, attorneys, and cash managers in Oregon, Washington, and California 10 times in 5 years.

CASH MANAGEMENT

Managed $110MM short-term investment portfolio for Company, a medium-size equipment-lasing firm, consistently exceeding benchmark portfolio yield by a minimum of 3%, while assuring corporate cash requirements were met.

Generated 5-year cash and portfolio yield projections for board of directors to use in strategic planning of equipment acquisitions.

EDUCATION

1967   AA, College of St. Martin

APPENDIX B: INSPIRATIONAL READING SUITED FOR IMPLEMENTING PLAN A

Burns, Bruce, MD. *Feeling Good: The New Mood Therapy.* New York: Signet Books, 1980

————. *The Feeling Good Handbook.* New York: Penguin Books, 1990

Gawain, Shakti. *Creative Visualization.* New York: Bantam Books, 1979

Gendlin, Eugene, Ph.D. *Focusing.* New York: Bantam Books, 1978

Jampolsky, Gerald, MD. *Love Is Letting Go of Fear.* New York: Bantam Books, 1979.

Roman, Sanaya, and Duane Packer. *Creating Money.* Tiburon, Cal.: H. J. Kramer, Inc., 1988.

Seligman, Martin, PhD. *Learned Optimism: How to Change Your Mind and Your Life.* New York: Pocket Books, 1991.

Shinn, Florence Scovel. *The Writings of Florence Scovel Shinn: The Game of Life and How to Play It; Your Word Is Your Wand; The Power of the Spoken Word; The Secret Door to Success.* Marina Del Rey, Cal.: DeVorss and Company, 1988.

## CHAPTER 8

OUT OF THE DANGER ZONE
ENJOYING A CRISIS-PROOF CAREER

It's never too late to be
what you might have been.
—George Eliot, English novelist

As he was accepting the American Comedy Award, George Burns, then age ninety-three, said, "The first half of my life has been good, and I look forward to the second half being even better."

I often wonder what is it about people like George Burns that so appeals to us, that draws us to them. I believe it must be their quality of being fully engaged with life, their willingness to entertain the possibility of the improbable. These people seem to have found their true place in the world and thereby make their lives appear effortless, playful, and meaningful.

When you craft a crisis-proof career, you are able to entertain the improbable and find your own true place through your work. The exercises throughout this book can provide the signposts to guide you in this journey. In chapters 2 and 3, you identified both external and internal sources of endangerment, explored possible reasons for your career crises, and began to pinpoint new solutions. In chapter 4, you examined the demons within—some of the pitfalls that may keep people from successfully moving through important transitions in their lives—and learned ways to tame or slay those demons. In chapter 5, you began expanding your horizons and creating new possibilities. In chapters 6 and 7, you learned about making those possibilities a reality, step by step, day by day.

The outcome of this process, pursuing the career you want and doing the work you enjoy, is the tangible result of the internal lessons learned while completing these exercises. Yet there are intangible benefits, too. For while people expect a good job and greater flexibility of choice from their crisis-proof career, few are prepared for the repercussions they experience in other aspects of their lives. Most people underestimate the magnitude of the adventure on which they have embarked.

These intangible results—a sense of personal fulfillment and engagement with life—derive from the fact that crisis-proofing involves our primary relationship to ourselves, defining our place in the world and the contributions we have to make in it. Most of my clients find that living by their own agenda—not their parents', their peers', their spouse's—changes not only what they do in their career but how they feel about themselves and the choices they make.

CRISIS-PROOFING SUCCESS STORIES

Each crisis-proof career is unique: the journey you need to take is entirely determined by who you are, where you begin, and where you want to end. In laying out their career plans, some people make relatively minor changes, while others make a radical break with the past and pursue a completely different direction. You won't know which is right for you until you've completed your Plan A and Plan B and made the commitment to begin.

In working with many clients over the years, I have heard countless success stories, each of them unique. My clients tell me that the exercises I have created were instrumental in their success—the secret to discovering the answers they needed lay in knowing the questions to ask.

Who Am I? — Sharon

When I met Sharon at the career workshop, she was senior vice president of a regional bank. Employed by the firm since she was sixteen, Sharon was panic-stricken when a rash of layoffs swept through the bank. "I wonder if there will ever be any security in my life," she told the group.

After the weekend sessions, Sharon took her materials and started work on crisis-proofing her career. *I began somewhat halfheartedly,* Sharon told me later. *I felt good having something concrete to do about my sense of panic, but another part of me wanted to avoid the whole subject. By avoiding it, I was hoping it would go away.*

Then I was passed over for the regional president's job; they gave it to someone younger. It was the first time I'd gone after a position in the bank and not gotten it. I was thrown into self-doubt. What was wrong? Wasn't I aggressive enough to let people know that I wanted the job? Didn't I sell myself well enough? People couldn't give me any good answers and that wrangled me.

I returned to the exercises with a new incentive and came across the question, "Who am I?" Good question, I thought. Answering the assessments, I realized I had always been an overachiever without a vision. I had defined myself entirely in terms of my title and association with the bank, and I based my self-esteem on my ability to climb higher within the organization. Now I was no longer climbing, and even my position at the bank was in jeopardy. So who was I?

As I worked further on the exercises, I discovered some things about me I'd never realized. I found that I love autonomy and having authority and control over other people and tasks. I wanted to spend more time getting to know myself better, so I wanted to work where I could make my own hours and be more independent. I also saw that I needed a results-oriented job where I could measure my income by my ability to take risks and make deals.

In comparing the Critical Job Factors Assessment with my present job, I was amazed to see how few of the factors were satisfied in my current situation at the bank. I decided that I wanted to transfer to a different part of the bank, maybe asset management. I had worked there a dozen years before and enjoyed it. When I went to my boss with this idea, however, he told me that I had to wait a year to transfer. I felt like an indentured servant. I could hardly contain my anger. My boss told me I needed time to cool off. He gave me a month without pay to "regroup," as he put it.

I took the time off and went to visit some friends in Massachusetts, thinking that a change in scenery would allow me to think things through. There I continued the exercises. When I did the Career Lifeline, it was easy to see that I was at a major intersection in my life and that there was no one to save me but me.

When I got home, I decided to start building my network. I looked up old friends who had left the bank and found other jobs. They helped me realize that there is a whole big wide world out there. I had been so busy pursuing my career at the bank that I had never considered other possibilities. It began to dawn on me that I had many options I had never considered.

After I thought things over, I came back to the bank and resigned. A few weeks later my boss called and said that the bank hated to see me go. He offered me a special assignment at the bank that he said might become permanent. Now I was in a quandary. I used the Double Checklist of Job Likes and Dislikes to make up my mind. Putting my thoughts on paper helped me think things through. I saw that I had made the right choice in leaving the bank and that there was no going back. I called my boss and said no to his offer.

In preparing to take the next step, the Free-to-Succeed exercise was most helpful in cinching my decision. I had always wanted to become an attorney. In this exercise I saw how feasible that possibility actually was. I became excited about the future I could create for myself.

I sat down and outlined my Plan A and found myself talking about it to others. When I told my old friends about my decision to become an attorney, they reminded me that even in high school I had dreamed of becoming a lawyer. This bolstered my resolve.

Talking it up helped me gain confidence and support. Without realizing it, I was networking my way out of banking and into a whole new realm of options and possibilities. I called colleges and universities for information about their programs. I attended informational seminars and met people like me who had left their jobs and were going back to school. For the first time in many years I was excited about my life and my future.

I set up a plan to get my education within my allotted severance time. First, I enrolled in an intensive course to pass the exams that would qualify me for law school. There were several people like me in there, and we started a support group while we were studying in the course.

I passed the intensive course, and three months later I passed the law boards. Based on my plan, I started studying and exempting myself from undergraduate courses by taking qualifying exams. By the time I got into law school, I had only one year left of undergraduate work to complete.

In my last year of law school, I networked into a firm of five attorneys and worked first as a researcher and assistant. We made an arrangement whereby they paid for part of my college education, too. When I passed the bar, I came to work for the firm full-time.

It's been six years since I left the bank. Within that time, I went from a frightened ex–bank employee to a woman fully able to stand on her own two feet. I learned so much in the process. For one thing, I discovered that I am a different person now from what I was at sixteen. My wants and needs have changed. Earlier, I felt lucky to have my career at the bank; they were doing me the favor. Getting passed over for the president's job gave me a chance to stop, reevaluate, and look at my accomplishments in a new light. I realized that I'd done a lot. I had many valuable skills that I could use in a variety of settings. They could help me wherever I wanted to go to grab that brass ring.

I learned that relying on others doesn't get you what you want. The bank wasn't going to rescue me from myself. And staying on at a job that doesn't offer what you need is worse than taking the risk and moving on. When I learned who I was, I discerned that I could create a vision and a plan for myself for the first time in my life. I took the initiative and it worked out great!

What Are My Skills, Gifts, and Talents? — Warren

At the career workshop, Warren drew an appreciative response from the other attendees when he wryly explained, "I'm a middle manager: middle-aged in midlife and midway to I don't know where." In his twenties, Warren had been full of vitality when he got a job at the airline company. He did so, he said, because "I loved travel; working for an airline seemed more satisfying than working for the insulation manufacturer where my father worked." Warren settled into his job, applied himself, and gradually made his way up to marketing manager. As the years went on, however, his enthusiasm waned and he grew restless. Warren began to hate, even dread his job. The pressure to perform seemed to be increasing as he saw the younger men and women moving up the ladder behind him, each one ready to step in and take his place for a lower salary.

Warren told me, *The pressure and my own stress led me to increase my drinking. My wife and I seemed to fight all the time, usually about that. Other times, we fought about my generally bad temper. If I wasn't happy at work, she'd say, why didn't I do something about it?*

Finally, when my wife actually threatened to leave me, I knew I had to take action. I took some time off work, resolved to find some answers to my problems. I went back to the materials I'd received at the career workshop and dug in. I began working on my Find Your Bliss Grid, my Critical Job Factors Assessment, and the Double Checklist of Job Likes and Dislikes.

I learned I had no business doing what I was doing. I loved to travel, not marketing. My management job involved meetings, staff accountability, deadlines, and quarterly reports. I couldn't care less about those. I liked hands-on things—rolling up my sleeves and getting my hands dirty. I wanted variety and new challenges on a regular basis. I wanted to be active. I loved the feel of tying sailor knots and gutting fish on the dock, not pushing paper on a desk hour after hour. So what was I doing at the airline? When I asked myself what I would do on the Free-to-Succeed exercise, I thought immediately of escaping to the Pacific Northwest for an extended—if not permanent— vacation. That was where my wife and I had met on a fishing trip. She was from Canada and it was always our favorite part of the country.

I began to play around with ideas of how to incorporate travel into my career. The travel business seemed like a perfect place to start. I made a list of all my friends in the tourist or travel business. I began getting in touch with them one by one and warming our acquaintanceship. I let them know about my desire to change my situation and asked for their assistance.

One morning, out of the clear blue, I was taking out the garbage and I nearly ran over this big burly garbage man. He stopped and looked at me in my jogging suit.

"What are you doing home? Shouldn't you be at work?" he said.

"I'm taking some time off to look for a better job."

The garbage man hoisted our overstuffed green plastic bags into his truck. "What are you looking for?" he asked.

"Something in the travel business."

He motioned with his broad shoulder. "You know the guy who lives down there on the corner? The one who has the overgrown lawn?"

I nodded.

"That's Bill Weber. He's president of some big travel company. You oughta talk to him," he said.

I thanked him and we parted.

That Saturday, I noticed Weber mowing his lawn. It was the perfect opportunity to go over casually and introduce myself.

It turns out Weber owned a large travel agency that worked the Pacific Northwest. He was very friendly and glad to help me. He introduced me to a friend of his who was looking for someone like me to be the manager of the agency for British Columbia Tourism in northern California.

I took the job and loved it. I was back in the travel business with variety in my life, some excitement. I got my free flights on the airline I used to work for. I could travel up to my favorite part of the world to fish.

Once I was out of the corporate world and working for a smaller outfit, everything about my life improved. I realized in hindsight that I had spent years measuring my success in life by my title with a big corporation. But that was my parents' measure of success and security, not mine. Fishing, traveling, and boating trips, they told me, were for vacationers and teenagers, not responsible adults. I believed them. All those years I went along thinking I was doing well because I had a title on the door, my own parking space, and a corner office with a window. But I hated it. It had nothing to do with my natural skills or talents. I made up for my lack of natural business ability through sheer hard work. But, I can admit it now, I was mediocre in that job. I wanted to do something at which I was superior.

When I stepped outside the corporate box, I realized that I could change my measurement of success. I could put aside others' expectations, measurements, and standards and begin living from the inside out. I discovered my creative edge and played it out. Suddenly life was fun again. Work was a pleasure. I stepped into the biggest vision that I could create for myself.

No job is perfect. So every time I started to get bored with what I was doing, I relaxed and visualized my ideal hour, day, week, or year. This practice gave me the resiliency to transform and reframe whatever was unsatisfying into the way I wanted it. Every time I did it, my vision expanded.

Gradually, I began to realize that even this dream job was just a *transition. I began to imagine myself eventually not traveling to the North Pacific, but actually living in British Columbia, on an island or on the shores of the Campbell River. We could sell the house, I told my wife, and move up there. The first time I said it, she laughed and called me a dreamer.*

That winter I took a trip to the Campbell River to check out a package tour we were selling. I stopped to eat at a restaurant near the marina. I overheard two guys talking about how the harbor master was going to retire. A thought flashed across my mind. By this time I was used to networking with everyone who would talk to me. So I introduced myself and joined in the conversation with these guys.

I learned all about the harbor master, the town, and the job. Talking it over with my wife when I got home confirmed my desire to go after the position. Amazingly, I got it! Six months later, my wife and I sold our home and moved up to Canada. We bought an attractive 2,400-square-foot house right on the Campbell River. After three years as harbor master, I began going out on fishing expeditions. I got my license and became a fishing guide—quite a different title from a few years before!

Last winter I was written up in a national travel magazine. When I took out a journalist to catch fish on the river, he was so impressed with my lifestyle and my story, he brought his photographer back with him on the next trip. I made sure they caught tons of fish, and he wrote up the story. Now everyone asks for me. My wife and I couldn't be happier.

I think it all started when I realized that success was doing what you're good at and really want to do. At the workshop you told us to follow our passion. So I did, all the way to the end of the rainbow. Every vision got bigger and bigger. The tourist agency, then harbor master, then fishing guide. If I could visualize what I wanted to do, I could do even more. If I could be resourceful, resilient, and network, I could find the place I really wanted to be, doing what I really wanted.

Where Do I Want to Make (or Continue to Make) a Contribution? — Bert

Bert was a management consultant traveling for his company and making big bucks. He had come to the career workshop because, despite his success, something important was missing from his life. The uncertain economy, however, made him afraid to pursue other options. "People tell me to hold on to my job, this is as good as it gets," Bert told the group. "I think they're right."

Later Bert told me, *I knew there was something out of balance. I enjoyed the work I was doing, but the job was taking a big toll. The traveling, the long hours. It was harder and harder to get on that plane every Monday morning.*

It all came to a head one day when I came home unexpectedly after a business trip had been canceled. I walked into the empty house and felt an overwhelming loneliness. It was like a punch in my gut. I provided all this, but I was a stranger. At that moment, I wanted to be with my wife and kids, but I didn't have a clue as to where they might be, I was so out of touch with their schedules. It was as if we were living parallel lives.

At the same time, major changes were occurring in my industry. Before, I could count on one major client to take up my billable hours. No one scrutinized me too closely. Now my goals were placed higher and higher. They forced out my supporter in New York and brought in this blustery guy headquartered in Chicago. He'd come up every few weeks and push our consultants around. Long-term relationships no longer mattered. How much money you brought in each month became paramount.

My wife, Kate, noticed how irritable I was becoming. The pressure was really beginning to tell. The moments of fun were the weekends. I'd go to my son's football workout, or my daughter's choir practice. Kate and I would sit and talk for hours.

So it was a blessing in disguise when my new boss called me into his office and let me go. I guess I saw it coming, but after so many years, I didn't expect to be treated that way. They let me use my office and gave me outplacement counseling, so I had some breathing room to find another job. It took me several months to get through the emotional slush: feelings of denial, despair, and anger that I'd accumulated toward my boss and his treatment of me.

In counseling I could see more clearly how important it was for me to stop missing out on my family and that I needed to integrate my work and home life. As I began doing the exercises, I found I had been doing what I wanted to do in my career on a day to day basis, but in a way and on a schedule that took away all my enjoyment. In My Next Ideal Career Situation exercise, I saw how much I wanted to get away from corporate life. I wanted to stop living away from home and making quotas for people who could only see the bottom line.

Kate, too, was ready for a change and wanted a career that would use her excellent managerial skills. Together, we each developed a Plan A and a Plan B. We took out an equity loan. With my portion, I fixed up my office at home, purchased the necessary software, and took some investing courses. I developed more business with my one client and began doing some investing on the side. In no time, it seemed, my Plan A was under way. For Kate, we bought a fixer-upper. Kate was the on-site contractor and managed the tradesmen. After the renovation, she would realize a tidy profit on the investment.

At first it was rough going, but Kate and I were each other's cheering squad. I knew we were doing the right thing. The answer to my career problem seemed so obvious then, but it hadn't been really. I'd stayed on with my company as long as I did because I had no Plan B. If I failed, I thought, there was no safety net. With Plan A written out, I could take the risk of going on my own because I knew I'd thought it through. I'd articulated my dream and built it in realistic increments. I was finally able to move in the direction I wanted with the courage I needed to make it work.

Often I think back to those days at McKinnon and Stills. It was a training ground for me, and I don't begrudge them, but my life now is so much more in balance. I work out of my home and my time is my own. Now if I want to go see my youngest daughter practice at a school recital in the middle of the day, I can take off work and do that.

I am making more money now than I made on salary and bonus, and I set my own goals. It isn't my style to work for the purpose of meeting arbitrary goals set by people who don't know me or value my contribution. Now, I work one-on-one with my clients and build lasting relationships. I am living the same values in my work that I practice in my family life, the ones Kate and I want to pass down to our children. My work and family life are now well integrated. It makes all the difference.

My crisis-proof career plan allowed me to trust my curiosity and take charge of my own destiny. It gave me the chance to learn and master new things in life. Kate and I took a risk and won.

What Trade-offs Must I Make? — Shaun

Shaun had two small children and a wife to support. Nevertheless, he chose not to keep his job when the energy company he worked for relocated to Detroit. It was not worth it, he felt, to move his family from California, where they were happy, to the Midwest, where they had no family or friends.

Shaun told me, *This layoff motivated me to make some long-range decisions about my career. Just finding a job that would support my family was no longer good enough. Without a larger picture of where I wanted to be further down the road, I might land another job only to be out of work again next year, or the year after that. This time, I wasn't going to settle for whatever came along. I was going to be very picky. I set about the crisis-proofing exercises to try to figure out what this plan might be.*

What helped me most was to develop a description of my Critical Job Factors Assessment and to stick to it very closely. The Today I Am exercise helped me realize that I liked the corporate world. When I thought about where I wanted to be in five years, I decided I'd like to work in a company that could afford me a career path to treasurer, perhaps even chief financial officer. The company had to be growth oriented so there was room for my advancement. The commute had to be reasonable—forty-five minutes or less. The company had to show some financial stability, no more layoffs or new presidents deciding to relocate.

My Plan A was very specific and led to a very focused outcome. My Plan B was to go back to banking if Plan A didn't work out in time to meet the family's expenses. At this point, I had been out of banking for two years. I didn't want to go back, although all my good contacts were in banking. I wasn't asking for a whole lot, or so I thought.

For a long time, it seemed there was only one job out there and it didn't have my name on it. My Campaign Progress Review showed me something wasn't working. Then I took stock of my network. I was still talking to too many banking people. So I began to widen my network beyond professional friends to include more personal contacts. I began to think of the contacts I had at church, in my recreational associations, and my children's school. I used to complain that having kids forced you to be part of the PTA, Brownies, and Little League network. Now I was glad I knew all those people. Most of those parents were very helpful to me in providing me with referrals.

Writing my resumé also helped me get focused. I targeted the financial skills I enjoyed and wanted to use, rather than my banking experience. And when I talked to others about what I wanted, I stressed these skills. Before long, a parent of my child's classmate gave me a referral at a large utility company. As I networked my way around the company, my ability to be very clear about what I wanted meant that people knew where to direct me. I received a lot of interviews with people who seemed interested in my set of qualifications. They interviewed me for the job I wanted as assistant treasurer. My networking had given me practice in creating a dialogue rather than simply allowing myself to be interrogated, so the interviews went really well. I was hired as an assistant treasurer at a subsidiary of the company, a very entrepreneurial venture. All my requirements were satisfied.

What worked for me was understanding what I needed and wanted and then holding out for it. I recognized that there are always trade-offs, but it is important to be the one to choose which trade-offs you make. The plan made me see that it was up to me to decide what I wanted and not to get discouraged or scared when it wasn't immediately available. Believe me, it was worth the wait. Last year I was promoted to treasurer. I couldn't be happier that I stuck to my plan!

LEARNING THE LESSONS

In retrospect, all of these people realized that the lessons they learned through crisis-proofing were bigger than the new job or greater than the career opportunities they gained. They discovered who they are, where they fit in the scheme of things, and the contributions they want to make in life.

Most career crises result from our failing to trust ourselves and the creative options we can generate. Instead, we blame our problems on the external situation and seek only external solutions. We become a casualty, and not an agent, of change. When we are ready to assume the leading role in our own life story, we move into a new phase.

Who am I? Sharon thought she'd found the answer to this question as a teenager when she went to work for the bank. As she matured, her responsibilities and recognition at the bank seemed to keep pace. Her midlife crises occurred because she'd never stopped to evaluate herself as an individual outside the context of the bank or to match the person she was. As a result, she stayed too long in a career that didn't offer what she wanted.

Warren was a square peg trying desperately to fit the round hole his parents had defined for him long ago. In trying to settle for what he thought he should do, he brought himself to the brink of collapse. He needed to answer *What are my skills, gifts, and talents?* The crisis-proof career exercises taught him to trust himself and to use a different scale by which to measure his happiness and success. As a result, he was no longer mediocre or merely midway—he followed his dream all the way.

For Bert, the question was *Where do I want to make (or continue to make) a contribution?* He was doing what he wanted to do but in the wrong setting and for the wrong people. Often we decide on a career thinking in terms of *what* to do, and less often in terms of *where* to do it. Where, as Bert found out, can be as essential to our satisfaction as what. Focusing on all the factors in our careers, including values, may allow us to make the shift we need to bring the whole into balance.

When Shaun recognized that there was more to a career than getting a job, he took a second look at the question *What trade-offs must I make?* The answer spurred him to take charge of his career rather than leaving it to chance. He set his own agenda and then stuck to it.

The assessments and exercises in this book give you the internal preparation you need to discover your own crisis-proof plan. It's important to complete all the assessments thoroughly, since you never know where the missing pieces may be hidden. When you do, you may see that some questions will have more relevance to you than others, perhaps, but that they work as a whole; all have something to offer.

It is my hope that these stories and all the other success stories related throughout this book, all of which are based on actual experiences, will inspire you to complete the assessments, work out your plan, and then follow the daily regimen that can see you through the implementing of that plan. As you do, here are a few tips to keep in mind.

The outer world reflects your inner reality. Your relationship with yourself will always be reflected in your dealings with other people. If you learn to appreciate your accomplishments, trust yourself, and feel that you deserve what you want in life, your experiences will reflect that self-confidence with positive feedback.

Gordon had been out of work for nearly four months when he went on an interview one Thursday morning for one of several jobs he wanted. The interview went well and Gordon was offered the job.

Promising to get back to them with an answer the next day, Gordon left to go on another interview he had scheduled. With the job offer in his mind, he was feeling at his most confident. The second interview went well, and it, too, ended with a job offer. Gordon had two more interviews that day, and by five that evening he had received no less than four job offers. His confidence and good feeling about his first offer made him virtually irresistible.

Transitions are the time we most need to focus on the journey, rather than the destination, and learn to enjoy the creative process. The best options are found in the process of becoming. As a society, we are especially goal oriented. Yet in pursuing a goal single-mindedly, you may miss the chance to learn about better opportunities or to arrive at a better solution. Give yourself permission to stretch out of your comfort zone; take small risks that will reinforce your confidence to take on bigger risks.

Don't be afraid to ask for help along the way. Everyone needs feedback, structure, and support. Life is full of ambiguous situations. We need to counteract its confusion by initiating the feedback, making the structure, and finding the support we need, as Sharon did. Trust that people will help you, if you let them.

No matter where you are in your life or career, the time to begin crisis-proofing is *now*—to anticipate your need and know the answers within yourself *before* reaching a sudden impasse or a transition in your career. Don't wait for the disaster. You can take charge to make even a good situation better, as Warren did.

EASY CRISIS-PROOF CAREER MAINTENANCE

Each of us is forever a work in progress. There will never be a definitive answer to what we want to be when we grow up because we will never be able to answer the question *Who am I?* once and for all. Our lives are a series of transitions, and it's important that we continually reevaluate our choices and decisions.

Like a fine automobile, a crisis-proof career requires regular maintenance. Every six months, take time to reevaluate whether you need to make adjustments in your life or career in order to stay on course. Remember that burnout and job dissatisfaction occur so gradually you may not even be aware of them until too late. It is much easier to address these problems *before* you start encountering trouble. Again, let's review the four questions that will always help you evaluate potentially significant changes.

Who am I?

Am I currently playing the role I want to play in my work life? If not, what's changed over the last several months? If your answer is no or if you are unsure, refer to the Satisfaction Indicator in chapter 3 to evaluate this further.

What are my skills, gifts, and talents?

Am I currently using the skills I enjoy, so that I am playing up my strengths and minimizing my weaknesses? If not, what's changed over the last several months? If your answer is no or if you are unsure, refer to the Find Your Bliss Grid in chapter 3 and the Visualization exercises in chapter 5 to evaluate this further.

Where do I want to make (or continue to make) a contribution?

Am I currently working in a setting I enjoy? If not, what's changed over the last several months? If your answer is no or if you are unsure, refer to the Critical Job Factors Assessment in chapter 2 to evaluate this further.

What trade-offs must I make?

Am I currently creating risks that are realistic yet challenging and maximizing the rewards and nourishment in my work life? If not, what's changed over the last several months? If your answer is no or if you are unsure, refer to the Complete Job Burnout Scale in chapter 3 to evaluate this further.

THE CRISIS-PROOF CAREER: THE BIG PICTURE

When I talk about a crisis-proof career, many people conjure up images of a single, perfect job guaranteed to carry them through to retirement—an ironclad contract with the best possible employer. Obviously, such jobs do not exist. In fact, the chances are that you will change jobs more than once even after you implement your Plan A.

Instead, crisis-proofing is a way to view yourself and interact with the world that enables you to transform a crisis into an opportunity and to accept change as the potential for growth and improvement.

The external reality may be the same—the options you choose to perceive and the manner in which you act on them are what make the difference.

Poet Dylan Thomas described the writing of poetry as the journey from darkness into light. I think this applies to crisis-proofing as well. In the beginning of the process, most people start by making choices based on survival, fear, and safety. These choices are dictated by external pressures, limited by negative thinking, and most often reflect others' expectations as much as their own. Through assessments, questions, and self-evaluations, however, individuals begin to meet different aspects of themselves, putting the pieces together, seeing these parts in a new way, or maybe seeing them for the very first time. At this point, an important shift occurs as people expand their horizons, learning to imagine and create new options. As they do, they begin to trust themselves. The choices they make reflect their creativity and seem to speak from the heart, from the whole self and not just the professional or wage earner. Instead of negative, finite choices dictated by external factors, their choices reflect the positive, infinite vision of the inner person. Their lives not only become satisfying and fulfilling, but even inspired. People whose work is chosen from a wellspring of inspiration and creativity have truly crisis-proofed their careers.

People frequently ask me, "Why didn't I do this when I was twenty? Why did I have to wait until I was forty-five to find out what I really enjoy?" I believe there are two reasons. The first is that as young adults just starting out, we come to our jobs to learn who we are, to develop our natural ability and learn new skills. We are open and ready to absorb all we can. The information and knowledge we gain during the first and second decades in the work world become the materials out of which the more mature adult can fashion a crisis-proof career.

The second reason involves our ability to assume risk and take on greater challenges. At forty, people begin to feel they have nothing to lose. They are willing to change their measurement of success and, having achieved a degree of mastery over their careers and their lives, are ready to explore new options.

When we dare to learn about ourselves, confront honestly the person we are, listen to the child as well as the adult, set our goals, and name our options, we can find our place in the world and discover that we are, at last, in the right place at the right time doing the right things. We are enjoying our crisis-proof career.

Whatever you can do, or dream you can, begin it.
Boldness has genius, power, and magic in it.

—J. W. von Goethe

An Invitation

Dr. Peller Marion offers workshops and seminars on the topic of crisis-proofing your career. For further information and a calendar of events, send a self-addressed, stamped envelope to:

Dr. Peller Marion
Peller Marion Associates, Inc.
388 Market Street, Suite 500
San Francisco, CA 94111